PRAISE FOR
A QUICK TING ON...

'Groundbreaking,' *The Guardian*

'Amazing,' *The Metro*

'Timely and needed,' BBC Radio 5

'Spearheaded by the hugely impressive Magdalene Abraha, the heartening launch of a phenomenal new series,' Mellville House

'There is nothing like this,' *The Bookseller*

'What better way to begin Black History Month than with the announcement of a book series celebrating Black British life?' *Bustle* Magazine

'Magdalene Abraha will launch her long-awaited book series, *A Quick Ting On…* it's brilliant,' *Elle*

'Exciting,' *Refinery29*

'The first ever non-fiction book of its kind', *The Voice*

'*A Quick Ting On…* is set to be behind some of the most exciting books.' *Stylist* Magazine

'A game changer,' BBC World Service

'Bringing Black Britishness to the fore,' *The Blacklist*

'How much do you know about plantains? Or Black British Businesses? Or Afrobeats? If your answer is not enough, that could soon be rectified,' *Evening Standard*

A QUICK TING ON...
...ABOUT THE SERIES

A Quick Ting On is an idea rooted in archiving all things Black British culture. It is a book series dedicated to Black Britishness and all the ways this identity expands and grows. Each book in the series focuses on a singular topic that is of cultural importance to Black Britishness (and beyond), giving it the sole focus it deserves. The series was inspired by everyday conversations had with Black British folk far and wide, whether that be in WhatsApp group chats, in person, on social media, at parties, barbecues and so on.

    A Quick Ting On is about providing an arena for Black people to archive things that they deem important to them and in turn allowing these explorations to exist long after we are here.

A bundle of joy, learning, nostalgia and home.

Magdalene Abraha FRSA (Mags)
xx

A QUICK TING ON...

BLACK
BRITISH
BUSINESSES

TSKENYA-SARAH
FRAZER

JACARANDA

This edition first published in Great Britain 2023
Jacaranda Books Art Music Ltd
27 Old Gloucester Street,
London WC1N 3AX
www.jacarandabooksartmusic.co.uk

A CIP catalogue record for this book is available from
the British Library.

Interviews edited for clarity and concision.

ISBN: 9781913090630
eISBN: 9781913090647

Cover Illustration: Camilla Ru
Cover Design: Baker, bplanb.co.uk
Typeset by: Kamillah Brandes
Printed and bound by CPI Group (UK) Ltd, Croydon CR0 4YY

CONTENTS

1

BRIT-*ISH* BUSINESS

'I want to be a neurosurgeon!' That is what I told my doting mother when I was just a tender six years old. Only the ancestors could know how I had any understanding of what a neurosurgeon was at that age. I suppose it could have been attributed to the fact that my older sisters Laverne and Lorna were obsessed with watching Casualty on BBC One. Then, at eight, I wanted to become a vet because 'animals were much more interesting than people.' At the age of ten, I changed my mind about that and decided to simply become a 'regular human doctor' after I learned that I would have to treat *all* animals, not just cute puppies. I was constantly changing my mind in true neurodivergent style, but luckily by the age of 14, I realised I had an aversion to blood. So, I settled on becoming a lawyer.

At 14, I was told by family members and teachers that everything had to be in perfect alignment. My GCSE choices would inform the A Levels I took, which would lead me to university, and into the career that I had chosen seven years prior. With hindsight and lived experience, I know that rite of passage that I was sold on, and that we still sell many young people on is skewed—but that is for another book.

At one point or another, I think all Black British girls, well my friends at least, all dreamed of becoming lawyers. We dreamed of moving to New York without any frontiers. We dreamt of ferociously fighting and winning every case put before us whilst dressed in Burberry and Gucci. We would fantasise about being part of the corporate elite we knew nothing about and drinking cocktails after work together. Then after having a trailblazing career, settling down to live extraordinarily heteronormative lives at 28 in California and have three children with a 50 Cent, Chip, Omarion or Devlin look-a-like. We all had very different tastes in boys.

Our parents, carers and teachers were avid cheerleaders of these plans. We were first-generation working-class girls who were the first to have a 'formal' teenage education and were set to be the first in our families to go to university. We were daughters of immigrant parents who worked hard as hospital porters, hairdressers, cleaners, shop attendants and civil servants.

We ate free school meals, and some days would not eat, but sneak our sandwiches out of the lunch hall in our Nike Just Do It bags to give to our other friends who we knew had empty fridges to go home to. Despite sociological praxis demonstrating consistently that the Black experience is not monolithic when I was coming up, success in traditional Black British households meant attaining good grades, getting into university, becoming a doctor, lawyer, accountant and more recently an engineer! For our immigrant parents and carers, who often came from low-income, colonially ravaged countries, success was rightfully framed in terms of one's position in society and how much social and economic security one could garner through education and work.

In his 1943 book *A Theory of Human Motivation*, Psychologist Abraham Maslow argued that all people have specific needs that can be categorised into a hierarchy of importance, which explains our caregivers' specificity in terms of the careers they wanted us to forge.

Maslow argued that humans have various needs, which can be classified into specific groups and then ordered in a hierarchy of importance. At the bottom of the hierarchy are physiological needs, essentially the things we need to survive on a basal level, such as food, water, and sufficient warmth. So, that would mean finding a job with a good wage that could provide shelter, food and clothing.

Next on the scale is security needs, which reflect the desire to have a safe physical and emotional environment. So, that would mean finding a job that had grievance procedures for discrimination, that maybe offers health insurance and a pension. Closer to the top of the hierarchy is a person's social needs, feelings of belonging, equity and self-esteem. So, that would mean being able to find affinity with your colleagues at work, win awards, garner respect from others and maintain a positive personal image.

Essentially, our caregivers drove us towards specific careers, as they could provide for those basic needs and necessities productively and securely. Becoming a doctor, lawyer, accountant and engineer in their eyes, was success in its finality. However, at the top of the hierarchy is the concept of self-actualisation, which can only be attained if all of the basic security, esteem, social and physiological needs are fulfilled. In short, self-actualisation is the complete realisation of one's potential and purpose, where you can focus on personal growth and development without compromising the other needs. Self-actualisation is a privilege that our parents and caregivers did not have, but one that they hoped to live vicariously through us, their children, when we became those doctors, lawyers, accountants and engineers.

The book *Exploring the Entrepreneurial Society* suggests that those who start businesses or break away from jobs in large corporations may be looking for ways to satisfy their self-actualisation needs.[1] But getting to the privilege of self-actualisation where you can start a business or leave a 'secure' job to do so was and still remains a barrier for many people, so it made sense why our parents and carers, coupled with the understanding of the challenges our Blackness would present did not encourage 'jollyfoder' or 'whiteman gwarnings' despite some being 'entrepreneurs' themselves.

Until this day, many of the older Black business folk I know do not consider themselves to be entrepreneurs. They say things like:

'I AM JUST A HAIRDRESSER THAT HAS A SHOP IN DALSTON MARKET.'
'I ONLY BAKE AND SELL RUM CAKES.'
'I JUST CLEAN PEOPLE'S HOUSES ON THE WEEKEND FOR EXTRA CASH.'

But, these are examples of entrepreneurship. However, they do not deem themselves as 'worthy' business folk either because they were marginalised into having to work for themselves or understand that in our capitalist society doing braids, cleaning houses or cooking are deemed to have 'no value.'

When I was at college I deceived myself into taking biology A-level, for what reason I do not know! But it became a ritual of mine to sit staring blankly at the pages of the textbook in the Science block hoping my knowledge would fall into place. One evening, and very on brand may I add, I started to cry quietly thinking about my impending exam failure when one of the cleaners offered to help me out. This cleaner shared that he had qualified as a top heart specialist in Rwanda and fled to the UK in 1994 with his family to escape the genocide. Upon his arrival, he discovered he could not get any work in medicine because, in his words, his 'papers are nothing to these English people.' Instead, he started a small cleaning business with his wife, which was a full-time success until the recession in 2011. He decided to take up work in my school to supplement their weekend earnings. He did not see himself or his wife as entrepreneurs.

My grandmother, who immigrated as part of the Windrush Generation with my mother in 1958, was a knowledgeable scholar, researcher, and teacher who faced the same challenges. Her skills were deemed untransferable, meaning that she had to re-pivot and became a hybrid cross between wellness guru, healer and herbalist to provide for herself and my mother at the time.

Stories like these are not uncommon, if you are the child of an immigrant or are close in lineage to those who are immigrants. You will be familiar with the harsh sacrificial exchange that they are often forced into when migrating to new Western countries to be told their degrees, their credentials, and their experiences did not count here. Many of our ancestors had to start again, their hard work and expertise became invisible, and entrepreneurship became not something you chose to do but had to do to survive.

My journey into entrepreneurship is similar but different. I was born and raised in the United Kingdom, but there were constant reminders that my state of nationhood and racial-ethnic identity will forever be at odds with one another. I would never truly belong. The nature of Black Britishness is oxymoronic. We can place the two words together, and of course, there are Black British folk that exist and experience those two states of being together—I am one of them—but it does not mean that those two words we thrust together do not mingle without friction, nuance and seclusion.

Black British folk and I alike are consistently asked what Afua Hirsch calls, 'The Question':

> If I were to single out the most persistent reminder of that sense of not belonging, it would be The Question. The Question is: where are you from? Although I have lived in five different countries as an adult, nowhere have I been asked The Question more than right here where I started, where I am from, in Britain... I can't be British, can I, if British people keep asking me where I'm from?[2]

Like, I understand why the glow of my skin would suggest a clime where the sun is constant all year round and where mangoes grow on trees. By looking at me, I get it. But I have been asked the question by people who have heard me speak, people surprised at how 'eloquent' I am. I have come to accept that even though Black and British are sometimes placed together, they are opposing identities. It is like standing in opposition to science, truly believing that water and oil can mix.

As a Black woman existing in the United Kingdom, I have experienced my fair share of microaggressions. Starting mainly when I stepped out of the colourfully eclectic cultural hub of home, Hackney, to start university. What was most interesting, is that I did not travel far, I went a mere 40 minutes to King's College London, a well-esteemed, Russell group university. I was in a class of over 100 students, and I was one of five very visible Black students. My university experience was not one of self-exploration but self-erasure. I felt like an imposter, which slowly consumed the psychological safety to be my true authentic self in my home borough of Hackney, but also within myself.

On my first day on campus, a fellow student broke the ice with small talk and asked me what type of food I liked. I told him: 'I like Mediterranean and Chinese food if it isn't my mothers.' Surprised by my answer he went on to ask me if I liked chicken and watermelon. At the time it seemed like an odd food combination to me, but two years later an episode of 'Family Guy' would teach me what I thought was strange as an innocently thought up food combination was in fact a racist stereotype.

I endured students referring to Black people as 'coloured' and the seminar leaders not correcting them. I had peers ask me if 'my people' had houses 'back home' or if 'where you are from are things as bad as they look on TV.' When things got really bad, I went to see a university counsellor who said 'they [my peers] don't mean any harm, things would have been different if you went to one of those revised polytechnics.'

I am British born, but it was clear to me that for these mostly privately educated ignoramuses, Black people were all the same. This hostile environment led to me withdrawing from fostering real connections at university. Whilst other students' experiences were filled with youthful fun and learning—my university experience was one of survival.

Over the years, universities in the UK have increasingly been criticised for their hostile and racist environments, specifically Russell Group and Oxbridge universities. But it is not just the institution of education that propagates such environments; my experiences did not occur in a vacuum. They hovered and followed me, like a nimbostratus cloud that refused to dissipate, into my internships, workplaces, dating life, experiences with the justice system and medical care.

I started my business mainly to get away from the trappings of existing in a white space. I wanted to create a business, build a team and make a product or provide a service that was thoughtful and meaningful. Where I could operate in my full authentic self, not have to code-switch or consider how the tone of my voice would be received. I wanted to rightfully take up space where I could express myself without that foreboding double consciousness.

The concept of double-consciousness was brought to us by Frantz Fanon in his seminal work *Black Skin, White Masks,* where he argues that life in a Black body is haunted and trapped 'between the disguises of the white imago and the anxieties of lived experience.'[3] Fanon explores the repercussions of being 'epidermalised'* or othered, and examines the hierarchical binaries between the oppressor and oppressed while analysing the psychology of colonialism—and by extension, the effects that colonisation had on the psyche of colonised subjects.

As I researched this book, it became clear to me that it is this othering of the Black communities in the globalised west that has fuelled the success and surge of Black Owned Businesses in the UK. Whether it be beauty, fashion, media or tech, Black people have taken a stand to serve their local and global needs, or because they had no choice but to start a business as a means of survival, financially and emotionally.

Black entrepreneurship is radical and repurposed strength and foundationally necessary. It is taking a chance on carving out freedom and success in a world that, through subtle dog whistles, tells Black people that they cannot succeed. Entrepreneurship is a chance to rewrite history and inspire a new generation with the representation that we did not see or have. Entrepreneurship symbolises the opportunity to recreate the narrative and oneself outside of the gaze and expectation of capitalist white supremacist patriarchal society.

---

*   Epidermalised simply means to be noticed as a Black person, or more recently person of colour. We cannot hide our ethnicity or race, which in turn makes it easier for those who exist in an 'epidermalised' state to be discriminated against.

It is about windows and mirrors. Scholars and community leaders always say the age-old phrase 'you cannot become what you cannot see,' asserting that people from marginalised groups do not pursue career or academic opportunities when they are not exposed to or physically cannot see such possibilities. For instance, sociological studies have found that when women (and women of colour specifically) do not see themselves represented in STEM*, they may internalise that such careers are not made for them.[4] The same goes for entrepreneurship and leadership.

If we want to have a stable and sustainable future as a global community it is important that we shine a light on this with a burning sense of urgency. Positive action is an imperative. There is no end to the benefits we reach as a society when we have diverse business owners and leaders. In the McKinsey and Company 'Diversity Wins' report, it was found that businesses that have gender diversity outperform their competitors by 25%, and those with ethnic diversity outperform by 36%.[5] Ideas do not pop out of thin air. They are mustered up by people.

The less homogeneity and greater mixes of cultures, ethnicities, genders, sexualities, ages, experience levels, educational backgrounds and lived experiences the more likely that when these people come together that they will come up with impactful, purposeful, innovative and creative solutions. With these solutions going forward to cater to marginalised groups whether it be through a service, product or internal workplace policies. This can be seen in all of the businesses of the Black British entrepreneurs that I have spoken to for this project.

---

*   Science, technology, engineering, and mathematics (STEM) is a broad term used to group together these academic disciplines. This term is typically used to address an education policy or curriculum choices in schools.

However, representation simply is not enough. Especially when it is one-dimensional, superficial, or not actually representative of the diverse blended intersections we have as Black people. It is great for folk to have a vista of Black British Business people to look up to, but it is cursory if we do not have the other elements to make our ideas, visions and businesses a success. We need equity-led access to networks and finance and also the liberty to lean in and make mistakes.

During my writing journey, some folk who are part of the Black community and a sprinkle of emboldened souls who are not have shared some charged, unsolicited and anti-Semitic reflections about the landscape of Black British business with me. Some said that 'Black people don't want to see each other win,' 'the reason why Black people are not influential is that we do not stick together like [other groups of marginalised people]' or that when 'Black people achieve success they abandon their Blackness, "the hood" and everything that comes with it.'

With my whole chest, I vehemently disagree. We do want to see each other win, we do stick together, and I forward that remembering your history or 'where you came from' has nothing to do with the colour of your skin but more to do with your character. We may not have the same socio-economic privileges of our white British middle-class counterparts. We may not have a friend whose dad owns a media company that we can intern at despite having no CV, or an auntie who can give us a small loan of £20,000 to start our business, but what we do have is a sense of community and our innate oral tradition.

Whether it is hair, clothing, food, education, business or

even romantic relationships, we are shouting about the good and not so good news—because essentially, at the core of it, we want nothing but the best for each other. The idea that we do not support each other is rooted in white supremacist structural ideology—so cut that thinking out, deadass.

Writing this book has been a whirlwind of a journey. One that began with Magdalene Abraha (the creator of this magnificent book series) and I chatting away at The Ace Hotel in Shoreditch (RIP) over scones and herbal tea. We spoke for hours about entrepreneurship, our mutual love for grapes and navigating life as young Black women in the West. After our conversation it became abundantly clear that this book (and the book series) was needed. We must archive our past, present and reflect on what our future can be. That is what *A Quick Ting On: Black British Businesses* does—it is an exploration of everything we are, everything we have been and everything we can be.

A central part of this book has been conversations with Black people, delving into stories known and unknown. I have been blessed to sit with (or zoom) some of the UK's finest Black entrepreneurs, thinkers and creatives, hearing about their journeys, struggles and successes. The common thread? Perseverance and resourcefulness. That was perhaps the best part about the book writing process, that I was able to speak to so many inspirational Black people who are all making a huge difference in the entrepreneurial space.

Over the course of the past couple of years the creator of the *A Quick Ting On* series, Magdalene Abraha, and I have spoken for hours on end, bouncing ideas about what this book would become and to finally see it come to life is really special.

Special thanks goes to the countless brilliant Black entrepreneurs I was lucky enough to speak to—from Sharmadean Reid MBE, Oswald Boateng OBE, Yomi Onashile, Peju

Obasa, Sadie Sinner, Andy Davis, Nathan Mallo, Darren Tenkorang, Nicole Crenstil, Rachael Corson, Jocelyn Mate, Aaron Wallace, Sharon Chuter, Khalia Ismain, Tobi Oredein, Josh Rivers, Nina Hopkins, William Adoasi, Chloe Robinson, Tobi Oredein, Liv Little, Sait Cham, Tommy Williams, Demi Ariyo, Abadesi Osunsade, Kike Oniwinde, Tendai Moyo and last but definitely not least the pioneer and national treasure that is Jamal Edwards.

This book is special because it shares and traces our Black entrepreneurial journey in the UK and abroad. Interestingly, upon reading it you will learn that in many ways the Black entrepreneurial journey mirrors the lives of Black people in the West.

So here I am. I write this book not as a doctor, lawyer, accountant or engineer—but as a young Black girl born and raised in Hackney. A young Black girl who would grow up to be an award-winning Black business owner. A young Black girl who would one day be asked by another young Black girl to write a book on one of my most treasured passions—Black entrepreneurship. Entering the business field has been by no means been easy, but I would not change these experiences for the world.

I hope you enjoy this read and take in the truly beautiful journey of Black British entrepreneurship.

2

THE HISTORY OF BLACK BRIT-ISH BUSINESSES

Black people have existed in Britain for hundreds of years. Our history is rich and vast, but is often subject to misinformation, half-truths and outright lies. One common misconception is that any African living within a European setting before the mid-19th century must have been enslaved under colonial rule with very few liberties. This is incorrect. The reality of Black life in Britain is far more expansive than mainstream British history likes to teach us.

There are many reasons for these misconceptions, but the main one is the globally entrenched narrative of Blackness in the West being fundamentally linked to the enslavement of Black people. This idea is propagated and promoted not only by the British education system but also by films, books and the media. It is why many disproportionately place the word 'slave' alongside Black people.

The word slave is actually derived from the Slavonic people of Eastern Europe. 'Slav' was meant to demarcate those who were enslaved in enormous numbers by the Holy Roman Emperor Otto the Great and his successors from the 10th century onwards. More than 1,000,000 white Europeans were enslaved in North Africa between 1530 and 1780, having been captured from the shores of England, Ireland, France, Spain and Portugal by Barbary pirates.[1]

Historical records show that Black people in Britain have existed since as early as the 12th century, but the growth of the British empire caused the numbers to grow exponentially during the 17th and 18th centuries.[2] There are even newspaper reports from 1764 that document a Black only pub located in Fleet Street.[3] This pub was believed to be a safe space for Black people and housed groups of 50-plus Black women and men who enjoyed dancing and eating the night away.[4] Yes, that is right, we were doing up shubs* in 1764! This is one of the first documented accounts of a 'community' amongst Black people in Britain. Approximately 20% of the Black population in Britain were women at this time, which meant that inter-racial relationships between Black and white people were more common than we would assume for that time period.[5]

Black and white people were not only having children, they also socialised together, glugged down ale and sang sea shanties at 'bawdy mixed-race hops'[6] where people of all colours roared and danced. This lack of segregation began to give birth to the vernacular of multiculturalism.

When it came to African people actually getting to England this usually happened in the following ways:[7] 1) They came from other countries in Europe that were home to a larger amount of African residents. 2) They were brought by English merchants as servants or slaves. 3) They were on board European ships that were captured by English ships.

It is believed that Black people made up around 1% of London's population in the 18th century,[8] so for all intents and purposes, they were an extreme minority, but their presence would become a major subject amongst the British elites. Or as my peers and I would say, Black people were living rent free in the mind of many white middle class folk.

Pseudo-scientific philosophical arguments from the likes of David Hume and Immanuel Kant had begun making the

---

*   House party or rave that has little to no space because it is packed.

rounds. In 1753, Hume stated that Negroes were 'naturally inferior'[9] to white people. In the 1780s, Kant suggested that grades of superiority and talent were based on race, with white people being superior.[10]

This was the environment Black people in Britain were living in, in the 18th century. You may think such a challenging existence would mean that Black entrepreneurship was a no-go area, it was quite the opposite.

Black British entrepreneurship is not a new phenomenon. For as long as Black people have existed in Britain so have their entrepreneurial endeavours. As mentioned in the opening chapter, for Black people, entrepreneurship has been an avenue to potential freedom in a racist world.

For example, in the late 16th century records show that a small group of Black Africans set up shop in London, founding multiple businesses.[11] Archives of Black British entrepreneurship can be found throughout British history, including the 17th and 18th century.

When it comes to Black entrepreneurship, much of the literature available is centred around the USA, missing out the cultural trove that is Black Britain. Thus, it is only right that we shed light on the rich entrepreneurial legacy of Black people in the UK.

JOHN BLANKE (FL. 1501–1511)

John Blanke, also known as the 'Black Trumpeteer',[12] is the earliest identifiable portrait of an African in Tudor England.[13] Based in London in the early 16th century, we only have the two images of him that appear in the Westminster Tournament Roll (1511), where he is pictured with very dark skin, holding a trumpet and wearing a turban. That is the full extent of our knowledge of John Blanke, but the turban suggests Islamic religious roots, and given Britain's expeditions at the time one can assume he is of Western African origin.[14] John Blanke was definitely not a slave and, given traditions at the time, historians have assumed that he came from a musical family.[15] The art of reading music and plainsong were crafts often passed down from generation to generation. Blanke was hired to play music for the higher echelons of Tudor British Society and was paid a wage of £12 a year, which was three times more than that of the average servant.[16] Blanke was notable, esteemed, talented and most definitely Black.[17]

EDWARD SWARTHYE
(BORN BETWEEN 1560–1562)

Edward Swarthye was a African porter who found his way to England in a ship under the command of Sir Francis Drake, an English explorer and slave trader. Swarthye is believed to have been recruited into the army to fight alongside the English during a raid on the Spanish port of Cartagena in 1586, which is now modern day Colombia. Swarthye returned to England in 1589 with notable sailor Edward Wynter, with whom he shared a close and discreet friendship. Many scholars have tried to use the life of Swarthye as an example of how Africans were treated as equals in Tudor England.

During a 1597 court case, Swarthye was called to give evidence after being accused of whipping his white colleague, John Guye, on behalf of his friend and employer Wynter. The fact that Swarthye was accepted as a witness in an English Court of law confirms that he had been baptised and shows that he was not considered a slave. The lawyers who interrogated Swarthye treated him just like the other workers in the Wynter household.[18] There are numerous records of African descendants who were baptised, and therefore free in London, Southampton, Bristol, Edinburgh and other places across the United Kingdom. These Black Britons were not servants, they ran for-profit-entities, they were trades people, expert tailors, shoe workers, patternmakers.

IGNATIUS SANCHO
(C. 1729-1780)

The first Black British business found in historical documents was run by Ignatius Sancho. Sancho was a composer and a successful retail entrepreneur who ran a chain of small grocery stores in London. It is believed that Sancho was born on a slave ship, his mother died when he was an infant and his father committed suicide rather than live in enslavement. After Sancho was orphaned, he was brought to Greenwich, London, and gifted to three sisters to serve as their property and slave. During what we can only presume was his early teens, he met the Duke of Montagu, who was impressed by his intelligence and encouraged the family to give him an education, gifting him books to read despite it being forbidden for the enslaved to have any remnants of education at the time.[19] Sancho would grow to become an avid reader, a lover of poetry and was also naturally musically gifted. By writing, publishing and selling his own music, Ignatius Sancho earned a successful living for himself and bought his freedom.[20]

In 1774, with his own savings and help from Montagu, Sancho, opened a grocery shop, selling merchandise such as tobacco, sugar and tea, at 19 Charles Street in London's Mayfair, Westminster. As a shopkeeper Sancho enjoyed socialising with his many acquaintances and customers, who included the likes of British artist Thomas Gainsborough, the Shakespearean actor David Garrick, violin virtuoso Felice Giardini, novelist Laurence Sterne, statesman and abolitionist Charles James Fox, who successfully steered a resolution through Parliament pledging to abolish the slave trade.

Sancho quickly became 'the extraordinary Negro'[21] and was the first known Black person of African descent to vote in parliamentary elections in Britain in 1774 and 1780.[22] From the pictures and manuscripts that survive today, it is clear that Ignatius Sancho was a respected and well-liked member of British society. Upon his death in 1780, he was worth more than £700, which is about £100,000 in today's money, and left £130 in his will as liquid cash.[23]

Posthumously, his letters were published in a book, which became an immediate best seller. Sancho critiqued the capitalist system of profit and exploitation that intersected with religious ideology. His writing called on and questioned the Christian consciousness and was later used as evidence to support the abolitionist movement. Not only was Sancho an artistic talent and business owner, but he paved a way to freedom for Black people in Britain.

GEORGE AFRICANUS
(C. 1763–1834)

Africanus was an employment agency entrepreneur and landlord. He grew up as a slave to a wealthy family in Nottingham, but later took on an apprenticeship and learned a trade as a brass founder.[24] At 21, alongside his wife, Africanus started a business which served as an employment agency matching candidates to suitable work and families. The business was a huge success and was active for more than 60 years. You can visit a plaque in his honour at St Mary's Churchyard in Nottingham, where George worked and lived nearby.

JOSEPH ANTONIO EMIDY
(C. 1775-1835)

Joseph Antonio Emidy was a West African born musician and was sold into slavery when he was 12 years old.[25] Believed to have been born in 1775, Emidy would go on to become a well known violinist and a pioneer of classical music.[26] As a child Emidy was brought to Brazil to work on the plantations. His master would later take him to Portugal to work.[27]

Emidy's love for all things music would permeate those around him, he would eventually be given a violin and lessons. Within a few years he learnt how to play the instrument well enough to be admitted into the orchestra for the Lisbon opera.[28]

Emidy would be let go in Falmouth, Cornwall, in 1799. By 1802, Emidy would get married and start a music tutorial business taking on music students in the area.[29] His musical resourcefulness did not end there as he became involved in the Truro concert in the early 19th century.[30] Emidy would go on to create a large musical network in Cornwall, eventually creating an orchestra.

CESAR PICTON
(C. 1755-1836)

Cesar Picton is understood to have been sold into slavery in Africa at the age of 6 years old. Picton would be taken to

England from Senegal and given to Sir John Philipps, a Welsh politician, in 1761.[31]

When his owner died in 1784, Picton received £100 in the will. Picton used the money to start a coal business in a house in Kingston, which he would call 'Picton House'. Sir John Philipps' daughters also left some money to Picton in their will and by 1816, he had used the money to buy another house which would also become known as Picton House.[32]

Picton died in 1836 as a highly successful Black entrepreneur, one that was respected and well known in Surrey.

REASONABLE BLACKMAN
(FL. 1579–1592)

Reasonable Blackman was a silk weaver based in Southwark, London, in the late 16th century. Believed to have arrived in London from the Netherlands, which at the time had a community of Africans. When a war between Spanish forces and Dutch rebels broke out in 1550, approximately 50,000 refugees fled the Netherlands, escaping to England—it is possible that Blackman was one of these refugees.[33]

We do not know much about Reasonable Blackman, but it was clear he was a successful silkweaver, as he was married and fathered 4 children whom he housed and provided for. His marriage and family, in those times means that he would have to attain some wealth to be a provider.[34] Not much is known about his wife, but historians assume she was white and English, in part due to the small number of Black people in England at the time.[35]

Blackman may have chosen to call himself 'Reasonable' to let potential customers know that the cost of his services were indeed 'reasonable'.[36] While Blackman's surname was likely due to his complexion, as surnames like 'Blackmore' were usually used by Africans residing in England.[37]

Blackman's silkweaver business came at a time where the silk trade was on the rise with silk products considered high end fashion. It is thus fair to assume that Reasonable Blackman was able to capitalise from this demand.

The people mentioned are just a few of many Black British gentry, business owners and inheritors of enterprise and fortune. We have been sailors, tradespeople, poets, and musicians. We married and had families. Black people have added to British society, business and politics longer than our history books care to document.

THE ENTREPRENEURIAL SPIRIT OF THE WINDRUSH GENERATION

In 1948, the 'Empire Windrush' would arrive at Tilbury Docks on the River Thames.[38] The boat was full of people from the British Colonies in the West Indies and would lead to the creation of African Caribbean communities in the UK. This moment started a never seen before Post War immigration story in the UK. The term 'Windrush Generation' is used to describe the West Indian Commonwealth citizens who migrated to England and Wales between June 1948 and 1971.[39]

This generation became midwives, nurses, porters, cooks, factory workers, ancillary workers and pretty much every occupation you could imagine.[40] They carved out lives from nothing, working hard in a very hostile and racist Britain to become homeowners and found successful Black-owned businesses.

Up until the Windrush scandal of 2018, very little was

known about this generation of migrants, which is shocking when assessing just how much they were responsible for in Britain. At the time of their arrival, Britain was significantly weakened by the impact of World War II and it would be the Windrush generation that worked to help to rebuild the country.[41]

Newly arrived people from the West Indies set up shop in the form of newspapers, magazines, hair salons, stores, radio stations, music companies, restaurants and much more.[42]

The entrepreneurial spirit of the Windrush generation would go on to permanently shape British food, music, politics and culture.

RESTAURANTS OF THE WINDRUSH

The Windrush generation dramatically changed the food scene in the United Kingdom. British food before mass migration lacked diverse flavour. Migrants from the West Indies, in search of their cultural cuisine and community, created local eateries that served staple dishes such as Rice & Peas, Jerk Chicken and much more. Many areas across the UK, such as Notting Hill and Brixton in London and Moss Side in Manchester, were rundown and dilapidated after World War II.[43]

Thanks to the new West Indian migrants who created restaurants and communal clubs, these areas were given a complete cultural makeover. Being that the UK at the time was a heavily hostile place for Caribbeans, these food venues became important spaces for members of the community to gather together and worked as a form of cultural retention for this community.

Eventually, the Caribbean eateries of the 1940s developed

into a large wave of Caribbean eat-in restaurants and social clubs by the 1960s and 70s. Restaurants, such as the well known 'Black and White Cafe' in Bristol, founded by Jamaican-born Betram Wilks, opened in 1971, Dougie's Hideaway Club and West Indian restaurant in North London, opened in the 60s and known for playing Calypso music, and the infamous Mangrove restaurant in Notting Hill, London, founded by Trinidad born Frank Crichlow in 1968 amongst others.[44][45]

NEWSPAPERS & MAGAZINES

A notable social entrepreneurial development of the Windrush generation was the creation of multiple Black-owned newspapers and magazines, most of which were intentionally anti-racist and anti-imperial publications. The British media landscape in the UK in the 1950-80s did not provide much space for Black voices, specifically those that were voicing the truth about the racialised society they were living in.

The publications worked to provide a voice and legacy to the Black British experience. Many of these publications gave a voice to Black immigrants, publishing updates and news from their nations of origin, working to provide a voice to the Black British experience of that time. The existences of such publications were not ordinary entrepreneurial expeditions, they were radical and extraordinary in every possible way.

These publications and their founders existed in a blatantly racist 60s Britain where there were no Black newsreaders or Black DJs on radio or TV. This was a time where there was only one Black footballer playing professional football (John William Charles for West Ham football club), Black people were regularly racially abused and often unable to rent due to tenants not wanting to live with a 'coloured' person.

At this time the British Union of Fascists would regularly have speeches in Brixton (yes, that's right, Brixton!) lecturing members of the public about the evils of interracial relationships. The slogan, 'Keep Brixton White' was regularly graffitied in Black areas and even found its place on an electoral campaign pamphlet for three candidates from Union Movement for the London County Council Elections of March 1955.[46] This was the societal landscape that Black people were living in.

The West Indian Gazette, also known as the West Indian Gazette and Afro-Asian Caribbean news, is believed to be the UK's first large Black newspaper.[47] It was founded in Brixton, South London, by Trinidianian born activist Claudia Jones in 1958. The West Indian Gazette published news from Black diasporic nations, updating those in the UK who were now away from home. It also featured Black poetry, stories and general literature.[48]

The West Indian Gazette's founder and editor Claudia Jones was an activist widely known as 'the mother of the Caribbean carnival in Britain.'[49] Jones's activism was large and expansive. In response to the Notting Hill Race Riots of 1958, which occurred just months after the West Indian Gazette began, Jones, helped organise the Mardi-Gras community carnival in St Pancras Town Hall, North London, in 1959.[50]

Jones would go on to organise numerous Caribbean Carnivals across London.[51] These events are widely seen as the start of what would eventually become the Notting Hill Carnival. Due to her notoriety as an activist, Claudia Jones is not often referred to as Black British entrepreneur but she certainly was one.

The Voice newspaper was founded in Hackney, by Val McCalla in 1982,[52] the Brixton Riots had occurred less than a year prior. The publication was unlike any Black British newspapers and magazines before it—with its targeted demographic being British-born Black people as opposed to Black immigrants which the Black British press usually focused on.

The Voice got started with a Barclays loan of £62,000, which was extremely uncommon at the time. Black businesses were very rarely able to obtain funding from British banks.[53] However, Barclays was on the receiving end of bad press due to their investments in apartheid South Africa. Due to the negative exposure, they were keen to invest in Black businesses. Upon *The Voice*'s inception, many did not foresee the success or longevity in a newspaper that focused on a British born Black demographic, yet today *The Voice* remains the only British national Black newspaper in the United Kingdom.

The Voice newspaper holds an impressive roster of Black writers in its alumni and continues to provide a space for Black British journalists to tell Black stories. *The Voice* paved the way for many Black magazines and publications proving that producing content for British born Black people is both societally and financially viable.

McCalla became a millionaire and moved out of his council flat to reside in the country.[54] He travelled back and forth to London in his Mercedes car but upon being repeatedly stopped by police on his travels, got rid of his Mercedes, opting for a Volvo instead.[55]

Flamingo was a Black British magazine founded in 1961 by Dominican-born Edward Scobie.[56] The magazine was created to represent the voices of the 350,000 West Indians, as well as the thousands of Africans and Asians, living in the UK.[57] The publication was diverse in terms of content publishing a range of short stories, long reads, cultural reviews as well as news.[58]

The ROOT is another Black-owned newspaper created by the Windrush generation, it was founded by renowned Black

British photographer Neil Kenlock, launching in 1979. It was the first Black British glossy magazine.

BLACK HAIR AND BEAUTY

When the Windrush generation arrived in the UK the Black hair industry was non-existent—from hair shops to hair salons, the provision of Black hair was nowhere to be seen. Considering the fact that the Black British hair industry is now worth tens of millions, this is quite a reality to imagine. On top of this, white hair salons at the time would frequently express their unwillingness to cater and tend to Black hair.[59] It was also challenging for Black hair dressers to get jobs in white hair salons or barber shops. The Caribbean community responded to this problem by setting up shop and creating their own salons, barbershops, hair stores, manufacturers and distribution companies. Some of these businesses operated out of people's homes, however, as time went on more and more Caribbeans would physically open up Black hair spaces.

Len Dyke and Dudley Dryden founded Dyke & Dryden Ltd in the mid-1960s. It was first a company that sold records until 1968 when Tony Wade joined the company, resulting in a switch in direction. What was this new direction? The Black hair and beauty market!

Dyke & Dryden Ltd became a juggernaut in the Black hair and beauty game, opening up their first hair shop in Tottenham, London, and eventually other stores across the UK Dyke and Dryden would become the first ever Black British million pound company. Like many entrepreneurs of the Windrush Generation, the brilliant trio regularly supported the Black British community.

In 1987, an American corporation called Soft Sheen

products purchased majority shares of Dyke and Dryden Ltd. With the change in ownership, came a change in how the business was run.[60] The new owners were not familiar with the UK market resulting in delays and issues that looked like the company was on its last legs. Eventually Tony Wade bought back Soft Sheen's shares, however, the company he took back was in a very different condition to the one that was initially sold.[61] Dyke and Dryden Ltd would focus solely on manufacturing, closing down their retail sections. In 1998 Wade would sell the company off, this time for good.

Dyke and Dryden left a strong and lasting legacy, reaching unheard of heights for Black British businesses. Len Dyke, Dudley Dryden and Tony Wade were three migrants from the Caribbean that permanently altered the course of Black British entrepreneurship in the UK. Dudley Dryden died in 2002 and Len Dyke in 2006. Tony Wade would go back to live in his home country of Jamaica.[62]

In the 70s hairdressing pioneer and Black entrepreneur Winston Isaacs created the Splinters hair salon. Isaacs, who became known as the 'Godfather of Black British Afro hair dressing', went on to teach and mentor some of Black Britain's most well known hairdressers to date, including but not limited to Derek 'DeCutter' Clement and Charlotte Mensah. Splinters was located in London's West End and is known as the first Black high-end salon in the UK. The salon was hugely successful with famed Black clients frequenting the salon to get their hair done—Black artists, Black politicians and even nobility from Africa all walked through Splinter's doors to get their hair just right.[63]

The Black hair industry would continue to grow, thanks to the Windrush generation and by the 80s it was no longer difficult to locate a Black hair salon or barbershop in Black areas across the U.K. Today the Black British hair industry is estimated to be worth £88,000,000.[64]

TRADING

Oswald 'Columbus' Denniston came to London from Jamaica in 1948 aboard the Empire Windrush.[65] Denniston, a respected member of the Caribbean community in London at the time, was known for his bubbly personality and entrepreneurial spirit. The 1950s would see Denniston open up a jukebox coffee bar called the Sugar Cane, in Brixton.[66] By the 1960s, Denniston would set his heights further, leading him to become the first ever Black trader in the UK. Denniston would begin selling materials and clothes in Brixton, making him the sole Black person in an industry that at the time was predominantly dominated by eastern and Jewish traders.[67]

Denniston did not stop there. He expanded his business, opening up and managing another stall in Brixton as well as three additional ones across separate London market places. Denniston's stalls became communal hubs for fellow Caribbeans to come along and discuss the day's news and musings. Denniston's love for community did not exist only within his business, he was also a founding member of the Association of Jamaicans at the Lambeth Community Relations Council and in the 1950s he became the first ever Black cyclist to join the Herne Hill Cycling Club.[68] Dennington was heavily involved in his local community, ardently supporting groups and individuals who also made strides in improving the lives of Caribbean people in the UK.

CHOICE FM

Choice FM became the UK's first Black licensed radio station in 1990 in Brixton, South London. Whilst the 90s were well after the Windrush period in the UK, the existence of Choice FM was the direct fruit of the Windrush Generation, founded by Patrick Berry and Neil Kenlock (also founder of the ROOT magazine) who are members of the Windrush generation. Choice FM became one of the most important media platforms for Black British people.

During its decades in function, the station championed Black music both in Britain and abroad. As well as creating space for musicians, Choice FM would give a platform to a generation of Black DJs and radio hosts.

Choice FM would also air debates on issues important to the Black British community that were not given a platform on other British stations and media outlets.

Capital Radio Group took full control of Choice FM in February 2004, moving the station to Leicester Square, London.[69] By 3 October 2013, Choice FM became Capital Xtra, ending it's strong and influential 23 year tenure.[70]

The entrepreneurial spirit of Patrick Berry and Neil Kenlock created one of the greatest Black British businesses of all time, with fruits that run deep in British radio and music today.

THE MUSIC INDUSTRY OF THE WINDRUSH

Another huge entrepreneurial contribution made by the Windrush Generation was an unquantifiable contribution to all things music in the UK. Music in the West Indies was already amalgamated with musical influences from Africa, Asia and South America, thus when the first of the Caribbean migrants landed in the UK they brought with them an enriching musical culture that would popularise a mass wave of genres such as reggae, calypso, ska, soca, dubstep, and even gospel, jazz and blues.[71]

The musical influence of the Windrush generation would also go on to strongly colour and influence newer genres such as Grime, drum and Bass and dubstep. Sound system culture originated in Kingston, Jamaica, in the 1940s. Sound systems were purpose-built, sonically loud and movable audio mediums that worked to play music publicly. Within Jamaica, holding dances and selling beverages centred around the sound system would become a popular and lucrative avenue for music lovers and DIY entrepreneurs alike.[72]

Sound system culture became the crux of Jamaica's music industry—the entrepreneurial skills of those sound system operators led to them being able to create music businesses. Sound system operators would provide space for music loving audiences, creating a circuit of makeshift clubs and raves.[73] To stay ahead of fellow competitors, sound system operators would go on the hunt for exclusive songs to play at the dances they would host. This entrepreneurial spirit would lead to a new type of music industry that would go on to reshape music across the world.

When the Windrush generation came to the UK, they imported their sound system culture. Caribbean musicians and sound system operators now in the UK would introduce music from the West Indies.

This music entrepreneurial spirit would also appear when Caribbean men and women began selling records in the UK. People would use their networks back home to import new music for the UK market. The selling of music did not always occur in record stores, rather it would occur in restaurants, cafés, clubs, stalls, hair salons and barber shops. The audience that purchased the music would in turn arrive at the sound system dances, breeding a self contained, effective business model that operated outside of the British music industry.[74] The organic and versatile nature of this model meant it allowed Black music in the UK to recreate and define its own sound and culture.

BLACK BRITISH ENTREPRENEURSHIP TODAY

We are living through an exciting time here in Britain. The current entrepreneurial landscape for Black British businesses means that there is a chance for true longevity in a way that has not existed before. As present day Black British entrepreneurs, we did not get here alone. We have all arrived here because of the hard work, resilience and determination of Black British entrepreneurs before us. Because of them, the road is one that has been tread on, waiting for us to add to it and reinvent the route.

Today, we have tools in our arsenal that our predecessors did not—from social media, the rise of e-commerce, globalisation, less barriers to education, access and so much more. This, of course, comes with its own set of obstacles and challenges. As a Black British entrepreneur myself, I know that it has gotten better, but the road ahead is still long. My hope is that Black British entrepreneurship can develop into a fruitful self-sufficient ecosystem.

3

SISTERS, DOING IT FOR THEMSELVES: BLACK WOMEN IN BUSINESS

OPEN YOUR WALLET

The business world is dominated by white men, making the inclusion of women, and even more so women of colour, extremely challenging. In 2017, former Chancellor of the Exchequer Philip Hammond commissioned a report undertaken by the British Business Bank in partnership with Diversity VC and the BVCA to identify the issues women-led firms were facing. The 'UK VC & Female Founders Report',[1] which was later published in 2019 highlighted just how bad it was *in these streets* for women founders. I knew it would be bad but even I was shocked by just how bad it *really* was.

The report found that all women founder teams in the UK ranked lowest when it came to raising capital. For every £1 of venture capital (VC) investment, women founder teams attained less than 1p whilst male founder teams received 89p and mixed-gender teams secured 10p. To add insult to injury, 83% of deals that UK VCs made in 2019 had no women on the founding teams.

Just as bad was the fact that 75% of all pitch decks that reached the VC firms had no women on the roster. The report also revealed that founding teams with at least one woman were less likely to get follow-on funding. 53% of teams with at least one woman got a second round of funding compared to

61% for all-male teams—and this difference persisted in each subsequent round. Then to top it off, teams with more women than men tended to receive unwelcoming and cold receptions from investors. Delightful!

There was one dimmed glimmer of hope in the report—venture capital investment for women founded start-ups were slowly increasing. However, for all-female teams to reach even 10% of all deals it would take roughly 25 years—so we are talking 2045 to see any real improvement. It is rough out here!

The 2019 'UK VC & Female Founders Report', by the British Business Bank, focused solely on the intersection of being a woman in business. So, what would the statistics look like if race was added into the mix? Black female founders are held back by an additional barrier which is often referred to as the 'Black tax'.

Originally founded in socio-racial theory, the phrase 'Black tax' was initially used to describe how race coupled with social-class robs an individual of their ability to build wealth from the moment they are born. The term is used to cover a variety of social and economical issues that impact Black people. It covers the way Black professionals are culturally expected to give prodigious financial and emotional support to family members. The way in which deep seated structural racism perpetuates a cycle of inequality such as lower pay and a lower standard of education for Black communities. It even extends to the way in which Black people are perceived as: 'less credible, less productive, less intelligent, less trustworthy, less sensitive, less deserving of respect, less human, just all-around less.'[2]

'The Black Tax' means that there is an inherent fear of investing in businesses led by Black people. Investors often hold these businesses to a higher standard than those founded by white men. Even once Black women appear to knock down the doors, they are detained at the threshold and denied entry. This pattern sees Black women having to go the extra mile to prove their value and worth in a way that their counterparts do not—this might include them having to get additional education, research and years of experience in order to mitigate the barriers set against them. 85% of the Black founding women I have spoken to whilst writing this book have been able to recount moments where their Black womanhood worked against their entrepreneurial endeavours. For example, having male members of the team deliver pitches so the company could be taken seriously all the way to women founders being mistaken for 'the assistant' at trade shows and events.

Over the past decade, across all the vast global pools of tech only 0.006% of funds have been granted to Black women founders.[3] This comes as no surprise, as psychologically people are drawn to those they have more in common with, which means investors are more likely to invest in those who share commonalities with them—which is usually other straight, 'educated' white men.

Before we continue, let me let you in on a secret about myself. I have a kink. Well, kind of. My kink-ish is that in my spare time, I like to find a company, scour trail Companies' House (United Kingdom's registrar of companies), research its founder, and find out how they built their business. Interviews with white male founders are my personal favourite, I usually save them for weekday evenings when I need something I can easily fall asleep to. You often get the typical, 'I had to work hard, my dad gave me £20,000 to prove the concept of X,' 'my uncle is a successful business man with a respectable portfolio of Y,' 'whilst studying at Oxford I met my business partner whose parents owned Z and they guided us' or sometimes, quite audaciously, some bozo who thinks he is the next Walt Disney but wants to sell water at pH 5 tells the world, 'my last business failed but this time I had a better idea, and they believed in me and trusted that I would make a return on the investment because of my passion.'

This is not hyperbole, there are *noted* receipts that were so long they made their way onto the big screen. Have you watched the documentary on Fyre Fest? Or maybe Inventing Anna? Not one Black founder that I know (including myself) has ever gotten investment, sponsorship or exposure with 'just an idea' or 'dream', let alone f*cking passion. The reality for Black entrepreneurs is very different.

Sharmadean Reid MBE is a British Jamaican entrepreneur, who was born and raised by her mother in Wolverhampton. She was the creative marvel behind WAH nails and was the air under the wings of Beautystack. Beautystack was an app that functioned as a professional beauty booking app with heavy focus on social content.

Have you ever been searching through hashtags like #nailsofinstagram and find the perfect set, take it to your local nail technician and they either flop the design or cannot do it? Well, Beautystack changed that experience, it even had an inbuilt booking system which made the whole experience from discovery to design effortlessly streamlined.

Reid has defied all the odds by being one of very few Black female founders to date who has been able to raise more than £1,000,000 in investment and in a conversation with me she shared how she has been able to circumvent the issue of raising capital. Despite already having proved her business prowess with WAH nails and Beauty stack, she was set, straight out of the gate, that she wanted to build a venture backed business that would make a return.

Firstly, Reid thought about the business she wanted to build and took stock of what she was passionate about. Essentially, 'if you do not enjoy the type of business you are building, you will not feel compelled to work the long hours it requires to make it a success.' Secondly, she researched the investors or type of investors she wanted for the business and from there was able to hone in on and truly understand what they meant by the term, 'success'. She learnt their 'language' and means of communication in order to produce a pitch deck that truly spoke to them not only financially but emotionally. Thirdly, Reid stayed true to *the* vision.

Adjustments were made where she thought they could make her business a more investable entity, but never once did she sway away from the vision to 'economically empower women and connect women from all across the globe.' In 2021, Reid launched The Stack World, an evolutionary pivot of Beauty Stack, for women who are changemakers, entrepreneurs and innovators interested in media that covers topics such as beauty, wellness, business and society. I have been following Reid over the past 8 years, and her face should appear in the business dictionary of what it means to be a lean entrepreneur.

Yes, of course, if you can authentically talk the talk and walk the walk, and back all that up with research you will be in for a win but Reid has transcended that. She consistently listens to the needs of her business, customers and the technological changes called forth by society that is never-endingly in flux.

What Reid does not know is that she is frequently on the minds of us Black girls on the come up. We talk about her as if she is a mythical being—because we cannot imagine doing what she does or pivoting the way she does with such thoughtful precision. It is inspiring. Then on top of it all, she is a charitable, doting mother who always makes time to mentor others and impart precious wisdom she has learnt along the journey. Reid is the definition of a compassionate leader who has not just defied the odds through hard work, but she gets up everyday and uses every opportunity to show us how to do it.

Despite the odds being stacked against us, Black women entrepreneurs stay moving, striving, fighting for a seat at the table, or we are carving the tables for ourselves. Year on year, Black women remain the fastest growing group of entrepreneurs across the planet[4], embodying the phrase 'f*ck it, I'll do it,' a proverb that should be solely reserved for Black women.

The rise of the 'sideprenuer' is a phenomenon that has become more noticeable in the past 5-10 years. Sideprenuers describe enterprising folk who run seasonal or part-time businesses whilst working full-time or part-time jobs to avoid taking money out of the cash-flow. Over the past five years the number of women sideprenuers has grown exponentially, with women of colour leading the charge.[5] The rates of sidepreneurship among women of colour are two times higher than all other businesses, and in 2019 it was noted that women of colour account for roughly 50% of all women-owned businesses. I am proud to be part of the new trend of Black female sidepreneurs that continues to grow at a global rate of 99% for Black women and 63% among Asian women, who are starting roughly 1,817 new businesses per day.[6]

I spoke to sideprenuer Yomi Onashile, founder of The Wig Bar London, who started her business because of the lack of high quality affordable wigs and hair extensions. The Wig Bar London helps women protect their hair investment by repairing, restoring and repurposing the wigs and hair extensions they already own. The postal wig and hair extension aftercare service not only extends the lifespan of hair extensions but also provides a sustainable solution to wig and hair extension waste. Onashile at one stage was running her business and working full-time whilst looking after her son.

Onashile, like so many other Black female entrepreneurs,

defied the odds by remaining focused on the end goal of providing customers a valuable and much needed service. For Onashile, the biggest challenge was finding a balance between work and all the other areas of her life, but now she cites decompression time as super important to her process, as it gives her mind the space it needs to allow creative ideas to grow.

Founder of the eponymous fashion brand Peju Obasa was born in London, but comes from a long line of strong Nigerian blood. Currently, alongside her part-time job, Obasa designs and makes accessories and ready to wear pieces using sustainable practices. The decision to work part time affords her the flexibility of spending most of the week working on the business and also means that she can continuously reinvest profits back into great products.

The brand is fortunate enough to have been able to take on an intern, which lends her even more time, when she is not working part-time, to continue designing and producing pieces, fulfilling orders, liaising with suppliers and marketing the brand. For Obasa, working part-time has allowed her to learn from an established business structure, which helps her run her business with a good idea of what works and what does not. When you are a sidepreneur, finding time for yourself is often a challenge, and this is something that Obasa struggled with for a long time before she decided that self-care had to make a regular appearance. By creating and setting up a clear schedule day by day, Obasa has been able to carve out space for herself. Discipline was a key word that featured throughout our discussion, and it is this discipline that has aided Obasa to consistently work efficiently.

Khalia Ismain, co-founder of the Black British discount card Jamii is another example of a Black British woman in the entrepreneurial space who has created a successful and smart business that serves her community. Jamii in many respects is a selfless endeavour, one that houses hundreds of Black British creators and entrepreneurs. The name itself comes from the Swahili word 'Jamii' meaning 'community' and that is at the core of the company's ethos.

Jamii's vision was to grow the Black entrepreneurial class and guarantee the discoverability of Black owned businesses throughout the UK and it has done just that. Jamii continues to expand, widening the amount of Black businesses it platforms but also importantly providing invaluable opportunities for Black businesses to not only exist but thrive. Crucially, Jamii connects Black businesses with industry experts working to demystify the world of entrepreneurship for Black businesses. To date Jamii have held multiple pop up shops in London and Birmingham, they have partnered with Airbnb to provide grants for Black businesses, they have provided Black businesses with billboard space and they even released a short film in partnership with Pinterest called *Legacy: Stories Of Black British Entrepreneurship*.

Ismain like many of the entrepreneurs in this chapter created a business to solve a problem her community was facing. Her entrepreneurial journey has led to Jamii cementing itself as a business that literally gives back to other Black businesses.

Black Ballad is a UK based lifestyle platform that seeks to tell the human experience through the lens of Black British women. The company was founded by Tobi Oredein in 2014 and came from what she describes as 'passionate frustration.'

Tobi Oredein studied American studies at university,

where she noticed that Black British culture wasn't as delineated as it is today. She was interested in what she calls the 'pillars in [African American] culture' from specified African American media to African American beauty brands and so much more. She was specifically interested in African American media and how they documented African American life. It caused her to ask, 'where is that in Britain?' a question that I think is asked by many Black British entrepreneurs across multiple industries.

On the topic of British media, Oredein laments that 'the media landscape is inherently racist,' a sentiment that I share. So what did she do? Oredein flipped the script. She applied for journalism and media jobs but she couldn't break through into the industry, noticing the girls who got the job all looked the *same*. Black girls have all been there! Realising that the reason she was not getting the jobs was not because she wasn't good enough or talented but because she didn't have the network, or a certain look. Oredein, like many of the Black British entrepreneurial women in this book, was a Black girl trying to get her foot in the door of an all white industry.

This gap between opportunity and Black women is a common thread in the entrepreneurial journey. Oredein's story in creating Black Ballad mirrors that of many Black women entrepreneurs. No one would give Tobi an opportunity, so she gave herself an opportunity to, in turn, give other Black women opportunities.

Today Black Ballad is a central hub for Black British womanhood, providing a viable and freeing space for Black women to express themselves. Oredein's journey highlights many of the structural issues we have explored in this book, ones that disproportionately hinder Black women in the creative and entrepreneurial world. Equally, Oredein's journey highlights the creativity and resourcefulness of Black British woman entrepreneurship. Oredein spoke to me about how important it is to her to provide opportunities for Black women, herself now taking a step back from editorial duties giving the space for other Black women to attain experience and careers. In a media industry where Black women are underpaid and under-valued—Black Ballad does the complete opposite.

'IN TERMS OF GAL-DEM, THE REASON IT HAS BEEN ABLE TO TAKE SO MUCH SPACE IS BECAUSE IT HAS PROVIDED A SPACE FOR OUR COMMUNITY TO TAKE UP SPACE TOGETHER'
—LIV LITTLE , FOUNDER OF GAL-DEM

Liv Little started *gal-dem* magazine as a student at the University of Bristol. Like many accidental entrepreneurs, Little had no idea just how impactful *gal-dem* would become but what was always abundantly clear for Little was the importance of community and unity in the development of *gal-dem*. Little spoke at length about the importance of *gal-dem* providing the freedom to explore topics in ways not typically offered in the media landscape.

Little came from a TV background where she saw the power of 'the networks that facilitate certain voices to be heard and uplifted.' Noting that 'there aren't enough people in positions of power who can facilitate our voices to take up space,' Liv created *gal-dem* to solve this very issue. Similar to Black Ballad founder Tobi Oredein, much of Liv Little's founding vision was rooted in creating opportunity for those who would find it hard to penetrate a challenging media industry. Today *gal-dem* is an award winning staple in the British media world, providing space and giving careers for important voices within the UK.

In order for us to understand Black women's place in the world of enterprise it is important to acknowledge the critical impact of social class, race, gender and culture in a historical context. We are going to leave the UK for a moment and look at Africa, where in some parts of the continent, women have been involved in business and trade since the 17th century.[7] It is important to understand that our notion of Black British woman-led entrepreneurship or Black woman-led entrepreneurship did not originate from, nor does it solely exist, in the West.

The term 'African Market Women' refers to women who are rural market traders in open markets usually found in villages and/cities in Africa[8] and interestingly in this industry, women traders are more populous than men.[9] Within this space, women hold more economic value, this is particularly important as the market system is a major economic network in most African countries. Historically speaking, these women would control the production and distribution of agricultural and craft products at a local level. Historical references show us in regions such as pre-colonial West Africa, when African women became highly successful creating trade routes for things such as gold, ivory and salt they would informally be known as 'market queens'.[10]

Today, the food economy within Africa exists through a system of multiple players all responsible for different parts of the chain. This includes, but is not limited to, street vendors, wholesalers, local and city stores, farmers, factory workers, retailers and traders.[11] Within this system the market trader, who is usually a woman, is an essential part of the chain.

The role of women traders has benefited from higher levels of development in nations or regions that were less disrupted by external violence, often in the form of land conquest, apartheid and things of that nature.[12]

'African Market Women' worked hard and smart to feed and support their families as well as contributing hugely to their local and national economies. Though this role is a working class role and many of the women traders are living below the poverty line, research has shown that in nations such as Ghana and Kenya, these women are able to exist in their societies without being financially dependent on men.[13]

Over time, due to globalisation, religion and modernisation the industry that women traders operate within has changed. Nevertheless even with the constant changes, the role of the African market woman has actually given the economies of African countries more grit, equipping them with the ability to be able to withstand war, natural disasters and political turmoil and other calamities.[14]

Black women's herculean contributions as leaders and business owners have not been acknowledged because history has always been framed from the position of white male grandeur, and Black women have historically lived 'in [the] double jeopardy of belonging to an "inferior" sex of an "inferior" race.'[15] To me it comes as no surprise that 'Black women have been central to the development of humankind since its inception,'[16] providing the framework of what it means to be entrepreneurial, but just like our contributions to art, culture and fashion it is conscientiously erased.

There are so many examples of Black women ruling, guiding and maintaining prosperous nations, industries and businesses throughout history.[17] A treasure trove of accounts of Black women successfully leading enterprises or business negotiations throughout history to the present day could be named. From Queen Hatshepsut, who ruled Egypt in 14 BCE and was responsible for pushing economics and science to guide Egyptian life and was known for using cooperation rather than competition to rule the nation.[18] All the way to Empress Eleni of Ethiopia (circa 14th century), who was a warrior, scholar, politician and strategist who used her enigmatic charm to maintain alliances which protected her country.

Not to forget iconic Black entrepreneurs such as Madam C. J. Walker (1867–1919) who is believed to be the first female self-made millionaire in America and built a hair and beauty empire through the Madam C. J. Walker Manufacturing Company, Maggie Lena Walker (1864–1934), the founder of the first bank in America to be owned by a woman, all the way to our modern day Black women entrepreneurs, the Bajan songstress and entrepreneur Miss Robyn Rihanna Fenty, who is now a billionaire due to her inclusive beauty and fashion empire, to our very own Black British beauty pioneer and icon Pat McGrath. The list is diverse and plenty—the legacy of Black women in Business is strong in success and numbers.

BLACK BRITISH WOMXN AND VC FUNDING

Right, so now back to Britain. Only 10 Black female founders in the UK received VC funding between 2009 to 2021,[19] so it only feels right to highlight some of these exceptional women:

TENDAI MOYO OF RUKA HAIR

Ruka Hair provides premium hair extensions that match Black women's curl patterns. In conversation with Moyo she shared that the world has benefited from Black women's innovation within the beauty space for too long without providing valuable solutions to their needs. Moyo started her business so that she could be part of the legacy where Black women feel represented, served and respected.

SIMI LINDGREN OF YUTY

Yuty is a sustainable AI beauty brand that offers personalised products to its users. European beauty techs have gained considerable traction in the past few years, and this year, Yuty secured £500k in a seed round led by Ada Ventures, after being bootstrapped for 18 months.

RACHAEL TWUMASI-CORSON AND JOCELYN MATE CO-FOUNDERS OF AFROCENCHIX

Afrocenchix sells hair care products for afro and curly hair, and in 2021 secured £1m in seed funding from Google, you can learn more about the company in chapter 5.

CHANTELLE BELL OF SYRONA WOMEN

Syrona is a pregnancy-test-like product that detects cervical cancer in women. It also has an app that offers gynaecological advice for people with a uterus by allowing them to track health symptoms, communicate with a community of users and get insights approved by doctors. Founded in 2018, Syrona first received £20k in angel investment from Bethnal Green Ventures. In June 2021, it received a $67k grant from the Boosting Female Founders Initiative.

NICOLE CRENSTIL, CO-FOUNDER OF BLACK GIRL FEST

Then we have the founder of Black Girl Fest, angel investor and all round babe, Nicole Crenstil. Not only has she managed to secure investment, but constantly pours back into her community with knowledge, mentorship and financial investment through Ada Ventures. I first met Nicole about six years ago. At the time I had just launched my first business *Wildabout Magazine* that helped young writers demonstrate their skills and build a portfolio, and she was in the process of curating

Unmasked Women—an exhibition channelling the Black British female experience whilst focusing on Black mental health.

WE ARE MORE THAN MAGIC

Despite the constant erasure of our contributions to the world, Black women have survived, preserved and thrived against adversity. This is the sentiment behind the whimsical term, 'Black Girl Magic'. Black Girl Magic refers to Black women's phenomenalism despite the extreme struggles they face. It reinforces the idea that Black women are inherently magical, strong and able to withstand all forms of suffering. Therein lies the issue with this term—suffering. A commonly celebrated facet of Black womanhood is the strong Black woman archetype that perseveres through pain and strife.

Though well intentioned, celebrating such an ideal works to dehumanise Black women and depict them not as ordinary people but extraordinary beings *all the time*. The truth is, Black women are ordinary human beings. But this is forgotten in a world that consistently pushes the memo that to be enough Black women must be excellent or magic. Do not get me wrong, I love the term 'Black Girl Magic' and all the descriptors it bestows on us such as: diligent, hardworking, strong, resilient—because we are all of that-but we are still just ordinary people.

Yes, it is true we have to work twice as hard because of our race, three times as hard because of our gender and even harder should we have any other diversities, but we should not have to. Constantly reiterating that Black women can handle all the misogynoir and still be a Meghan Markle, a June Sarpong, a Serena Williams, a Michelle Obama, a Pat

McGrath and so on only works if we highlight and lobby that they should not have to!

As I have said, we are moving mountains, booting down doors and crafting tables so that we and other women like us can take a comfortable seat, but 'many Black women find it hard to admit that they are overworked, overwhelmed'[20] as historically we are everyone's 'passive nurturer, a mother figure who gave all without expectation of return.'[21]

Knowing this, I call on all my Black female entrepreneurs to take a moment of pause, and to look for ways to make each other's journeys easier—because sure as hell, no one is going to do it for us, but us. We must do it for ourselves and each other.

IT ISN'T JUST ALL BUSINESS

Black women encounter challenges inside the workplace. Not only do they have to combat the issue of patriarchy, but also have to navigate systematically racist workplaces at the same time. Black women are hugely under-represented in senior roles in the workplace. The 2020 Fawcett Society's 'Sex and Power Report'[22] highlighted the lack of ethnic minority women across top jobs in all sectors. Baroness Ruby McGregor-Smith, in her review 'Race in The Workplace', found that people of colour are more likely to be overqualified than their white colleagues, but white employees are more likely to be promoted.[23]

The 'Gender and Race Benchmark 2014', noted that Black women are the group least likely to hold executive or non-executive directorship positions despite the fact that Black women are twice as likely as white women to be leaders in their community—leading a youth initiative, heading up a community or charity organisation. Black women are also more likely to be the primary breadwinners in their families but their experience outside of work falls off the radar of 'management at work'.

Which is why it is no surprise that the Trades Union Congress (TUC) found that 45% of Black women felt that they had been singled out for harder or less popular tasks at work, with around one third reporting being unfairly passed over for or denied a promotion at work. Moreover, the report found that around 1 in 8 Black women working in the UK are employed in insecure jobs compared to 1 in 16 white women and 1 in 18 white men. The TUC says that many of these roles are in vital front-line services like health and social care, which ties into the fact that during the pandemic Black staff were at higher risk of COVID-19 exposure and job loss.[24]

In conversation with a Black woman leader in a blue-chip pharmaceutical company who asked to remain anonymous she shared that:

> 'It has been nothing but a struggle to the top of the chain. I have had to assimilate in ways that have made me feel like a sellout at times. For over 10 years I worked hard, "played the game" and now I am in a position of power where I can enact real change and make sure Black women do not have to struggle the way I have.'

There are a variety of ways Black women can help each other climb ladders and shatter the double glazed glass ceilings of the business world but being able to get yourself in a position of power seems to be a key way to create change. But that can be a tough, lonely and often exhausting road that is why the responsibility should not, like it always does, fall on the shoulders of Black women. Organisations need to do more to ensure that their hiring practices are fair, and that there is an open and inclusive culture in house. I understand that 'feelings' and 'culture' are often not put to the forefront in business, so let me promote diversity in a way capitalists might understand:

- Harvard Business School found that inclusive and diverse businesses are more productive and 70% likelier to capture a new market

- Over just three years, companies that have a highly inclusive culture notice 2.3 times more cash flow per employee

- Inclusive companies are 120% more likely to hit financial goals

In short, it pays to be diverse.[25] So if a company wants to boost the number of Black women at a senior level there are a few things that can be done immediately:

1. Suitable mentoring and training can be deployed to enable Black women to reach their full potential at work.

2. Examine employers' recruitment and retention policies and highlight this disparity.

3. Start employee resource groups (ERGs) that develop guidance and policies on supporting Black women in the workplace and to place equalities at the heart of the bargaining agenda.

A company I worked for was extremely open with their diversity statistics and shared them with all employees. They highlighted the lack of representation and came up with robust measures on how they were going to tackle the absolute lack of Black women in senior positions. They introduced an interview guarantee scheme, which meant that if a Black woman met the minimum requirements for a role they were offered an interview with a diverse panel which was made up with different genders, races and ages; if they were not successful at the interview stage then they were given personalised comprehensive feedback. And you know what happened? The representation of Black women at senior leadership level grew. So it is that simple. Change can happen, but there has to be a willingness to do so.

This is not to say that there will not be challenges on the road to business and organisational change, but to all my Black sisters reading this, I want to remind you that the power of great queens and warriors exists in you. You are the blueprint of what entrepreneurship and leadership means. Your craftiness, the ability to turn nothing into something, is rooted in the rich history of Black women who came before you. The world may not recognise you or your greatness yet, but I do, and your ancestors do—so start the business and go for that promotion, sis. You are 'entrepreneurship' and leadership defined.

4

INTERSECTIONS MATTER:
BLACK BRITISH LGBTQ+ FOUNDERS

Intersectionality is a critical framework which calls for us to look at the ways in which one's overlapping identities and experiences change the complexity of the prejudices one faces in the world. The term 'intersectionality' was coined in a groundbreaking paper for the University of Chicago Legal Forum by civil rights activist, lawyer and leading scholar in critical race theory Kimberlé Williams Crenshaw. In the paper, Crenshaw wrote that traditional feminist theory failed to recognise the plights of Black women and the overlapping discrimination that was unique to them. Crenshaw's intersectional theory affirms that people can be disadvantaged by varying different sources of oppression due not only to their gender as traditional feminist thought argues but also by their race, class, religion, sexual orientation and other identity markers.

Intersectionality as a framework took the world by storm, articulating what many of us knew and felt. The concept seems simple, right? I mean, of course one's experience and existence in the world is informed by the range of identity markers one holds. Yet despite the clear logic of it, much of the world's politics, institutions and cultures do not incorporate intersectional thought into their frameworks, which means we are often left with what can only be described as a hot mess!

Here are some examples of what happens what we do not think through an intersectional lens:

- Leading white women of the suffrage movement like Susan Anthony openly rejected the civil rights movement proclaiming: 'I will cut off this right arm of mine before I will ask for the ballot for the Negro and not for the woman.'[1] Going further, the suffragettes heavily opposed the passage of the 15th Amendment to the constitution in 1870, which nominally gave Black men the vote as they were against putting 'the ballot in the hands of your Black men, thus making them political superiors of white women' because 'never before in the history of the world have men made former slaves the political masters of their former mistresses.'[2]

- Articulations from liberal feminists such as actress Patricia Arquette who said in her 2015 Oscar speech: 'It's time for *all* the women… and all the men who love women and all the gay people and all the people of colour that we've fought for, to fight for us now.'[3] Rhetorically rendering women of colour, queer women of colour, and queer white women as somehow not of fitting into the category of 'all the women.' By referring to 'all the women'—but not actually encapsulating the experiences of all individual groups of women.

- Roland Emmerich's 2015 movie *Stonewall* embarrassingly erased and minimised the role that Black LGBTQ+ people played in the Stonewall Riots. The movie depicts a white man throwing the first brick at police, when it was indeed Marsha P. Johnson, a Black gay activist. This plays into the ways in which whiteness, and by extension maleness, is consistently positioned alongside leadership and more grossly resistance. Marsha P. Johnson's actions that day were radical not because of the act of throwing a brick—I mean, people have been rightfully bricking agents of enforcement for centuries—but it was their Blackness and marginalised identity that made the act revolutionary and radical. The erasure of Johnson was intentional, and speaks to why intersectionality is such an important politic to consider and understand when we talk about identity.

- In 2017, French cosmetic company L'Oreal, made the decision to fire transgender and Black model Munroe Bergdorf, as she publicly critiqued the violent white nationalist protests in the American city of Charlottesville expressing that all white people have to be accountable in talking about racial violence. L'Oreal was willing to use Bergdorf's identity to sell products and a message, but when it came to standing behind and up for oppression they chose to lean into the oppressive structure instead of listening and amplifying her intersectional voice and unique experiences on their powerful and global platform.

Intersectionality is an important framework for understanding how and why systems of oppression work. In an article on intersectionality in *The Independent* newspaper, the author states, 'All women do not have the same story, the same body, the same sexuality, the same experiences.'[4] intersectionality in turn 'takes into account the varying systems of oppression that interlock and result in unique experiences for women within the world.' By doing this, it works to give a voice to *all* women and consequently 'decentralis[ing] the dominant narrative of liberal feminism as the uniform voice for all women.'[5] This framework can be applied to any identity or intersection of identities.

Throughout this book, I have discussed the topic of business and the intersection of Blackness and national identity. But what about those entrepreneurs who are British, Black and LGBTQ+. What are their experiences? What are the barriers to entry?

Under the politics of intersectionality, those business leaders will face a sundry of obstacles, which will, in turn, affect the way they as people are seen in the business world and their businesses themselves.

LGBTQ+ ENTREPRENEURSHIP

The contributions of the Black British LGBTQ+ community in the UK are large and diverse yet these histories have not been given the recognition they deserve. Black British LGBTQ+ artists, activists, writers and entrepreneurs have pressed their fingerprints into the cultural DNA of Britain.

Some of my favourite historical examples of Black LGBTQ+ entrepreneurship include the fearless Pearl Alcock. Alcock was born in Kingston, Jamaica, and would come to the UK as part of the Windrush generation.[6] Alcock was a bisexual women and wanted to provide a safe space for the LGBTQ+ community to freely socialise with each other. In 1977, Alcock would open an unlicensed bar in the basement of her already existing clothing shop on Railton Road in Brixton.[7] Her bar was located near another pub called 'The George' that was known for not serving Black and/ queer customers.[8] Risky as it was to open up such an enterprise, Alcock did so motivated by the desire to serve and help her community.

The Black Lesbian and Gay Centre Project (BLGC) opened in London in 1985, after receiving funds from the The Greater London Council (GLC).[9] The group were committed to highlighting the racism that Black LGBTQ+ groups faced within the mainstream queer movement. When the GLC was scrapped, the Black Lesbian and Gay Centre had to rely on donations. In 1986, they started their own magazine called *Blackout*.[10]

Today, in the UK alone, LGBTQ+ purchasing power stands at £6,000,000,000 per year and it was not until the 1990s that terms like the 'pink pound,' 'pink dollar,' or 'pink economy' gained traction. The term 'Pink Pound' was first seen in the UK in an 1984 article in *The Guardian*, but before the 1990s, the world seemed not to acknowledge the massive contributions that LGBTQ+ folk made to the world of business and the economy.[11] It was coined the Pink Pound as historically, the pink triangle has been used as a symbol for the LGBTQ+ community, but it must be mentioned that it is shrouded in a dark history.

The pink triangle was created by the Nazis in World War II to stigmatise LGBTQ+ people[12] in a similar way that the Star of David was used to propagate the violence and subjugation of Jewish people.[13] The pink triangle functioned as a tool of Nazi oppression before it was successfully reclaimed many decades later by queer communities throughout the world.[14]

This reclamation saw the commodification of the 'LGBTQ+ lifestyle' by business leaders who were not part of the community, and then naturally by the LGBTQ+ community themselves who felt safe and comfortable enough to 'promote' themselves. The late 1980s and 90s are where the UK saw its biggest boom of the LGBTQ+ scene, and in 1984 gay entrepreneurs formed the Gay Business Association, whose express aim was to serve the gay business community.[15]

As someone who runs a fashion brand who stands in allyship with the LGBTQ+ community, authenticity is important. At my fashion brand, we demonstrate this authenticity by continuously lobbying for the rights of our LGBTQ+ siblings, we donate selected profits to LGBTQ+ charities and I make a point of hiring senior members of staff who are part of the community themselves.

But, sadly, when the spending power of the LGBTQ+ community was revealed, many brands jumped on the bandwagon of 'pinkwashing'. The term pinkwashing describes a business or brand who appears to be LGBTQ+ allies for positive public relation reasons, when in fact they actually are not.[16] For example, Heinz pulled an advertisement of two men kissing after receiving a slew of complaints from various dry, unmoisturised anti-gay groups. Or, the USA retailer Target, who ran an advert in the USA featuring a gay couple, but were later found to have donated cash to an anti-gay politician in 2011.

Or, the various companies, who cannot be named for legal reasons, donning the pride flag every pride month but continuously providing a hostile work environment for LGBTQ+ employees. Just a public service announcement from me to any business leaders who are reading or listening, if you do not live the message of your brand or believe in its politics do not bother because you will be found out. Do not be disingenuous and dark sided for the sake of capitalist profit—ew.

LGBTQ+ businesses make up less than 1% of businesses registered. Now, it is unclear why this is but I would hazard a guess that many business owners may be reluctant to disclose their sexual orientation and/ gender identity because of the largely homophobic and transphobic world we live in. According to Gallup, Generation Z, are more likely to disclose and most likely to proudly identify as part of this community, and I hope that in coming years with more awareness and visibility, we see the growth of LGBTQ+ businesses at scale.[17]

The Harvard Business Review argued that LGBTQ+ led businesses are generally more successful because they centre diversity, equity and inclusion[18]—which in turn means that they are able to attract top talent and show an active willingness to innovate to the needs of society. Yet despite this, LGBTQ+ led businesses are not represented anywhere as well as they should be, of course this also means the case is even more dire for Black LGBTQ+ led businesses.

A paper called 'African American gay male entrepreneurs: a study of enabling and inhibiting factors impacting entrepreneurial success' by Floyd H. Hardin III from Pepperdine University provides qualitative research with interviews from Black Gay business men living in America.[19] As far as academic literature and research goes, the area of LGBTQ+ entrepreneurship is limited and once you account for race, it is even more scarce.

This paper gives insight into the experiences of Black gay business men specifically those in leadership roles. What is clear from the paper is that both racism and homophobia play a large role in how the participants and their businesses are perceived. One respondent, for example, explained that, he had to be twice good as his white counterparts and that being gay added an extra layer that meant he always ensured he was 'proactive' and 'overprepared'.[20] This anecdote touches on what was similarly explored in Chapter 3—the added burden on those who have intersectional identities from marginalised communities results in them having to be exceptional to simply get in the room (and even that is not guaranteed).

Similarly, some participants within the paper believed their success in the business world was due to what they described as 'overcompensating'. One was quoted as saying, 'We often have to fight society's reaction to us because we are both Black and gay.'[21] With another expanding on the topic, stating, 'I am a dark complexioned, gay man. I always felt I needed to do more and be more.'

The intersectional identity of the Black gay men interviewed for the paper highlights the extra obstacles that Black gay entrepreneurs can be subject to before even getting into the challenges of actually running a business. On the topic of identity, one participant stated, 'as Black men, we always have to be on our A-game. We are Black first and then gay.'[22]

The stereotypical perception of Black people and homosexuality impacted many of the participants' entrepreneurial experience. One entrepreneur was quoted as saying, 'We continually have to fight the stereotypes of being both Black and gay. The media and society at large depict us as diseased, dishonest and disloyal.'[23] Another respondent expressed, 'I am a minority in many instances, and faces in my field don't look like mine. I have to be twice as good to get mediocre contracts than my white male counterparts.'[24]

The results of the research are not surprising and perfectly convey just some of the challenges that Black gay entrepreneurs face when entering the business world. The business world is simply a microcosm of the wider world—thus the most marginalised groups within society become the most marginalised groups within the entrepreneurial world.

The traits of being resourceful, nimble and creative are ones you find in Black entrepreneurship. Whilst this is something to be celebrated, it is important to note that this is born out of the disproportionate barriers to entry and success the Black community face within the entrepreneur space. Simply put, if we don't help ourselves, no one will! The 'African American gay male entrepreneurs' paper touches on how over time LGBTQ+ entrepreneurs are increasingly praised on their innovative skills and as a Black female entrepreneur I know that this is skill that we develop out of necessity. Being uniquely creative, innovative and resourceful comes from having doors shut on you and the constant lack of opportunity. Within the Black LGBTQ+ business world, a perfect example of this innovativeness is the National Black Justice Coalition in America. The National Black Justice Coalition are a civil rights group that supports and advocates for Black LGBTQ+ members in America.

In 2021, they created an app called the The Lavender Book.[25] The app works as a directory, listing businesses and locations within America that are safe spaces of LGBTQ+ people of colour. Taking its inspiration from 'The Green Book' a guide of safe spaces for Black people during the Jim Crow era. The Lavender Book is a perfect example of how members of the Black LGBTQ+ community are using their entrepreneurial skills to develop technology and business to protect the LGBTQ+ community of colour.[26]

UK BLACK PRIDE

UK Black Pride is led by the powerhouse that is Phyllis Opoku-Gyimah, also known as Lady Phyll. Apart from leading UK Black Pride, Lady Phyll is a political activist and the executive director of Kaleidoscope Trust, which is a nonprofit organisation that campaigns for the human rights of LGBTQ+ people in countries where they are discriminated against.

The main driving force behind the birth of UK Black Pride, like many Black-led businesses, was necessity. All intersectional communities struggle to grapple with the concept of race, and oftentimes there is an erasure of the experience of the Black experience. Racism has always played a role in relationships between white and Black queer people—with the main point of contention being the consistent whitewashing surrounding the movement for LGBTQ+ rights.[27]

Just as the movement for LGBTQ+ rights has been whitewashed, so has Pride month, which 'often feels like a white, gay-centred event'—far removed from the leaders of the Stonewall riots. People like Stormé DeLarverie and Marsha P. Johnson, alongside the names of other Black queer and transgender people who were on the frontline of the Stonewall Riots in 1969, are erased from the memories of Pride. It was these people, in their marginalised identities, that drove the movement forward for LGBTQ+ people across the globe to celebrate their identity every year.

The erasure of Black contributions to the Pride movement, as well as necessity, was one of the driving forces behind the establishment of UK Black Pride. Phyll wanted to create a haven where her community could come together to connect and express the vibrancy of their identities free from the gaze, judgement and racism of dominant cis-heterosexual society—they have carved out a celebratory, safe space for Black LGBTQ+ communities.

UK Black Pride began in 2005 as a day trip to Southend-on-Sea by members of the online social network Black Lesbians in the UK (BLUK), since then it has grown and expanded to include all folk part of the LGBTQ+ community. I remember first becoming acquainted with UK Black pride in 2018, when I attended their event in Vauxhall Pleasure Gardens, where more than 7,000 people were in attendance. To date it is Europe's biggest celebration for LGBTQ+ people of colour. UK Black pride are responsible for numerous events throughout the year with its signature event during pride month.

Their events are rooted in promoting emotional and spiritual health and support for their community. UK Black Pride is perhaps not seen as a business in the way that some other companies we have delved into but it is just that. UK Black Pride is a community business that works with a variety of entrepreneurs to effectively create a powerful space for their community.

Josh Rivers, creator and host of the award-winning podcast *Busy Being Black*, argues that institutions like UK Black pride demonstrate 'how creative, entrepreneurial and resourceful queer Black British people have been since day one.' Rivers was part of a group that founded Series Q, a network for LGBTQ+ entrepreneurs. Series Q's main concern was data from the Human Rights Campaign that revealed that more than half of LGBTQ+ college graduates went back into the closet when they entered the workforce. Additionally, the findings exposed that young LGBTQ+ people had reported seeing bullying and harassment: 70% had witnessed incidents motivated by race or ethnicity, 63% had seen incidents motivated by sexual orientation, 59% had seen incidents motivated by immigration status, and 55% had witnessed incidents motivated by gender.

Series Q were 'mortified' and wanted to explore the intersectional experiences of those who existed within multiple identities. Rivers started to interview people at Series Q events, and would explore how their experiences shaped their life and career decisions, going further to think about 'how they harnessed their passions to create change.' In 2018, Rivers launched *Busy Being Black*, a podcast exploring the fullness of queer Black lives and shared that 'the LGBTQ+ community has been full to the brim of entrepreneurs. Whether they think of themselves as such is perhaps less important than the real work they do creating space, visibility and recognition for our communities.'

Just before our conversation, Rivers interviewed Adem Holness, who founded the 696 music festival. The 696 music festival's name was inspired by a London Metropolitan Police form that club promoters were required to fill out before they could host an event. Rivers shared, 'the form asked questions about the type of music that would be played and the intended audience, and—surprise!—ended up being a tool to police and restrict Black gatherings. I say that to say, the obstacles we face will be much the same as Black Britons have faced and continue to face: they are structural, embedded and pernicious.'

We went on to discuss the disavowal of systemic racism in the 2021 Sewell Report. UK Black Pride alongside other LGBTQ+ charities provided guidance and evidence, but these offerings were intentionally erased. Just as in this instance that 'the intersection of race and sexuality is overlooked and disregarded, so will Black LGBTQ+ entrepreneurs face this type of erasure of their lived experience, too.' Despite all of this erasure, we had a great discussion about the social power of the Black community and the ways in which 'the founders of Twitter did not know they had a viable product until Black people got their hands on it.' Social media has been a profound tool, especially in our hands, so it is important that we promote Black-led businesses and services.

In Rivers' words, 'there has been sustained attention on our communities since the murders of George Floyd and Breonna Taylor, and the global uprisings that erupted afterwards, leav[ing] a lot to be desired. While I absolutely welcome any increase in business for Black creators and entrepreneurs, I would love to see a more rigorous and honest confrontation with systemic racism and homophobia. Some of us may well be able and empowered to run and build our own businesses. Many more of us will be prevented from doing so. How do we ensure that as many of us as possible have the means, access and opportunities we deserve?'

K Bailey Obazee, founder of PRIM, a digital story telling platform run by 'Queer + Black fam' based in the UK has an answer for this. There must be initiatives backed by investors, banks and brands to support queer-led businesses to be even more equipped to take up partnership opportunities, seek and secure long-term funding and, of course, manage the administrative side of the business better.

Black British LGBTQ+ entrepreneurs, 'need people to value [their] work and businesses beyond the possible short-term financial returns and to be more open to including queer Black entrepreneurs in conferences, business workshops.' As Obaze put it, being a Black, LGBTQ+ entrepreneur is a 'constant state of trying to remind [oneself] that queerness is an asset and not a challenge.' Obaze launched PRIM to make the stories of African, Caribbean and Afro-Latinx folk accessible to all, as at present there is no 'significant support network that takes note of our intersections and challenges as a result of that.'

Sadie Sinner is the founder of The Cocoa Butter Club, which is a performance platform that uplifts creatives, harnessing the idea of a network. The Cocoa Butter Club celebrates performers of colour, many of whom are queer, from all walks of life. Mixing spoken word, aerial displays and drag, its showcases serve as one big fabulous reminder that Black and brown cabaret artists not only exist but are here to stay—with flair.

In 2015, there were no Black lesbians booked for the cabaret stage for PIL (which has over 1,000,000 visitors). When Sinner enquired about this, she was told that there were 'no Black lesbians in cabaret,' so how could they be booked? There is an irony in telling Sinner, herself a Black artist in cabaret and LGBTQ+ nightlife, that she and others like her did not exist.

At the core of it, 'the people creating the shows were not going to the spaces to find Black and non-white talent' so she brought the horse to water and created 'a showcase as a way for event producers to discover talent for their shows.' The Cocoa Butter Club became *the network*, and since its inception Sinner has been nominated for a *Gay Times Honour* and was featured and supported by *Kurt Geiger*, for their *Power Empowered Campaign*.

Now, that is not to say she did not face systemic barriers, but the rallying behind the mission from publications such as *Qx Magazine* and *Attitude Magazine*, and venues such as *Her Upstairs* provided opportunity to spread the enterprise's mission and purpose. In relation to allyship, as Sinner puts it, 'consistency is key in the support you give.' Whether it be 'a like or share on social media, or a monthly donation, or spreading the word; allyship is an active effort.'

gal-dem magazine, an award winning media company, founded by Liv Little, was set-up by and for people of colour to share the perspectives of those from marginalised genders and sexualities. When *gal-dem* launched, it was about taking up rightful space. There were no 'outlets or networks that facilitated, upheld or uplifted people of colour let alone gave space for the other parts of their identity whether it be gender, sexuality, class or ability.'

When Little started on her journey of entrepreneurship she 'never envisioned where the business would have ended up... with part of that being testament to the community showing out, the fantastic team and allies who were intrigued with [*gal-dem*'s] offering.' In an interview for the book, me and Liv discussed how our communities will always show up for one another. Through *gal-dem*, Liv Little created a business that was rooted in community and connection—bringing together writers of colour and all of their intersectional identities.

In the UK today Black LGBTQ+ owned businesses and their founders are more visible than they were in the 70s and 80s, but there is still a very long way to go.

Black LGBTQ+ business owners and their businesses are not monolithic. When it comes to the statistics available, here in the UK, it is difficult to find solid statistics and research on LGBTQ+ businesses and entrepreneurs let alone Black LGBTQ+ businesses and entrepreneurs. The US is better, but even then, they are nowhere near the level they should be. What the minimal statistics do show, is that being an openly LGBTQ+ owned business is not easy. The business world needs to do better when it comes to making space for LGBTQ+ entrepreneurship.

Allies and the world of business must adopt 'respect for [their] personhood and work.' When you're working to build a business, having people around you that not only support you but genuinely understand your experience, people who can respect your boundaries—pronouns, sexuality, gender or non-conformity has a significant impact on well-being, engagement and creativity overall. In the words of Obaze themself, as allies we should 'keep buying, keep promoting, visiting the website and engaging in the content and events [LGBTQ+ folk] produce.' Everything is about numbers and the more people f*ck with it, the more it grows—it's that simple.

Here are just a few brilliant Black British LGBTQ+ owned businesses making an impact on the communities locally and globally:

AZ MAGAZINE

AZ Magazine is an online platform created by four Black queer women in 2015. *AZ Magazine* was founded to create space for LGBTQ+ Black people and people of colour, carving out a place where their voices could be heard, amplified and shared.

BBZ

BBZ London is a curatorial and creative production collective born, raised and based in South East London with roots in nightlife and clubbing culture. Prioritising the experiences of queer womxn, trans folk and non-binary people of colour in all aspects of their work, they provide physical and online platforms for this specific community.

OKIN EPIDERMIS

OKIN is a vegan and sustainable hair and beauty brand that uses ethically sourced ingredients. They aim to combat the harm the beauty industry has inflicted on the environment. The company uses 100% unrefined Shea Butter sourced from Ghana.

AFRICAN RAINBOW FAMILY

African Rainbow Family supports LGBTQ+ people of African heritage and the wider BAME community. The company was established in 2014 to support refugees and people seeking asylum, stand against hate crime and campaign for global equality especially in African Commonwealth countries where anti-gay laws seek to criminalise LGBTQ+ people.

BLACKOUT UK

BlackOut UK was created to recognise the need for Black queer men to have a space to think, shout, show off, curse, celebrate, launch, reflect, share and be heard. They encourage and stimulate debate and discussion online and face to face through their website, writer workshops, networking events, and supporting interventions to meet the needs of Black queer men.

EXIST LOUDLY

Exist Loudly is an organisation committed to creating spaces of joy and community for queer Black young people. Their work has included the first-of-its-kind research looking into the lives and experiences of Black LGBTQ+ youth in the UK within education, healthcare and the home.

JAY JAY REVLON'S 'LET'S HAVE A KIKI' BALLROOM PARTIES

Jay Jay Revlon is bringing back vogueing to London, by centring the Blackness and queerness of the movement from the 1980s and 1990s into the present day. Throughout Revlon's career, their events have raised money for many charity organisations that support QPOC and LGBTQ+ folk.

BLACK LGBTQ+ THERAPY FUND

Black LGBTQ+ Therapy Fund was set up in response to the worldwide pandemic, this was set up to fund therapy sessions for Black LGBTQ+ people, recognising the unique challenges Black LGBTQ+ people face and the huge mental health toll this can have. The fund initially asked for £1,000 but they were able to raise over £70,000 to fund a number of therapy sessions.

5

'BLACK IS BEAUTIFUL':
BLACK BRITISH BEAUTY BUSINESS

The phrase 'Black is Beautiful' gained traction amidst the Black power movement of the 1960s. However, the sentiment of the phrase has its origins in the mid-1800s, first noted in a speech in 1858 by John S. Rock, who was born a free slave in New Jersey in 1925. Rock was one of the first African American doctors in the United States, practising dentistry for more than ten years before moving onto general medicine, then later studying law after what he describes as having 'heard the groans of my people and am come down to deliver them.'[1] Later, Rock passed the bar in Massachusetts, and was in turn the first African American to argue cases in front of the United States Supreme Court. For Rock, he '[came] not to bring peace, but the sword… break every yoke and let the oppressed go free.'[2] He didn't stop lobbying for freedom—you were a real one John.

Though Rock did not utter the phrase, 'Black is Beautiful', on that fateful day at Faneuil Hall in 1858, his speech 'I Will Sink or Swim with My Race' highlighted the value, intelligence and beauty of African Americans.[3] Rock's clear message about the beauty and glory of Blackness in all its forms was a strong statement that would vibrate through the American and global Black community many years after his speech. It would in fact give birth to a cultural affirmation and political proclamation that would withstand time. James Brown's 1968 hit 'Say It loud—I'm Black and I'm Proud' perfectly demonstrates the phrase's permeance in popular culture, and how it seeped into the psychology of the Black Power Generation.

'Black is Beautiful' spread through the Black diaspora to confront the white supremacist notions that natural Black features are undesirable and lack aesthetic value. The movement asked Black people to stop lightening their skin, straightening their hair and other forms of nuzzling natural Black features,[4] this in turn led to a boom of the afro hairstyle as a symbol of the authentic Black self, as well as radical approaches to how Black people practised caring for one's appearance, namely via hair and skin. For some added context, during enslavement Black people were denied the right to hygienic items, grooming supplies, with adequate clothing often being restricted.[5] So when slavery was abolished, Black people invested in making themselves feel and look more aesthetically valuable, which surreptitiously led to beauty and grooming being a cornerstone of the Black community in the West.

Sarah Breedlove, more commonly known as Madam C. J. Walker, is believed to be the first female self-made millionaire in America. In the 1890s Madam C. J. Walker would develop a scalp disorder which resulted in the loss of some of her hair. Curious to understand and remedy the situation, she began creating and experimenting DIY remedies alongside purchased hair products.[6]

In 1905, Madam C. J. Walker would get a job under Annie Turnbo Malone in Denver, USA. Malone herself was a famous Black hair product entrepreneur, who is believed to be one of the first African American women to become a millionaire.[7]

While working for Malone, Madam C. J. Walker and her husband began producing adverts for the hair product that Walker had been creating. In 1907, Madam C. J. Walker and her husband began promoting her hair products throughout the South of the USA. Part of the promotion included Walker demonstrating what would become known as the 'Walker Method', which involved using her formula and hot combs.[8]

The success of Madam C. J. Walker's hair business led to her opening up a factory and a beauty school in Pittsburgh in 1907. By 1910, Madam C. J. Walker Manufacturing Company became a juggernaut in the hair care industry amassing profits that would be equivalent to millions of dollars today.[9]

Madam C. J. Walker's entrepreneurship and resilience without a doubt was the beginning of the commercial Black beauty business in the West, contributing to the ever growing £5,000,000,000 Black beauty industry that we have today. In the 1960s, thanks to the grit and resourcefulness of the Windrush generation, Britain finally saw its own Black hair and beauty trailblazers, Jamaican-born Lincoln 'Len' Dyke and Dudley Dryden founded the eponymous Dyke & Dryden which became the UK's first afro hair care distributor and first Black-owned multi-million pound business.

When starting out, Dyke and Dryden saw the trend of leading Black hair and skin product suppliers coming out of the United States, so they began to import goods from the likes of New York, Chicago and Atlanta. They understood what Black people wanted, and by 1989 they had six outlet stores developing some of the most top-selling products of the era, whilst increasing employment in Brixton and Tottenham for Black people. So what happened? Why are we not buying our products from a Black-owned hair stores like Dyke & Dryden today?

If you are a Black person in the UK, it is no secret that most of the hair shops we purchase our hair products from are not Black-owned but Asian owned. A notable one that you may have heard of or shopped in yourself would be Paks Cosmetics—a chain Black hair and beauty store that can be found across Black populated areas in the UK.

In the 1980s, it was common for Black-owned businesses to move forward with processes of mergers, collaboration and investment to secure the global expansion of their business.[10] As mentioned in Chapter 2: The History Of Black Businesses Chapter, Dyke & Dryden fell into that category. If you want to know more about the story of Dyke & Dryden's expansion and subsequent end, check out Chapter 3.

Just as Dyke & Dryden were synonymous with Black British hair care in the 1980s, Paks has now taken its throne. The South Asian community's entry into the Black hair industry is not new. For years Black hair products have often been produced and manufactured in Asia and by South Asians. Their visibility in the industry, namely due to their shift into the retail space, however, is a more recent development.

Peter Mudahy, CEO of PAKS Cosmetics himself, is on record stating, 'it's business'[11] and that South Asian dominance in the Black British hair industry is not a cause for concern, however, for Black consumers, the reality is much more complex than that.

So why and how is the Black British hair store market no longer dominated by Black people and specifically dominated by the Asian community? Well there are a combination of reasons but here are some key ones:

> **1.** Manufacturing and technical infrastructure: Manufacturing is a central part of any supply chain. When considering that plenty of Black hair products are produced by Asian manufacturers, namely South Asian manufacturers, it makes sense that this community is able to build successful stores selling the products they manufacture. This in turn equips them with the ability to purchase products in bulk at

low prices or build their business around their already existing businesses for example, owning a factory producing hair products and then opening a store to sell the products that the factory produces.

2. Retail infrastructure: South Asian retail businesses in the UK were successful, solid and developed for some time. The application of their already existing business model to the Black hair and beauty industry was seamless and effective in a relatively short space of time.[12]

In the UK, we spend about £1,200,000,000 a year on our hair and beauty, with Black British women spending six times more on beauty products than their white counterparts, despite making up less than 4% of the population.[13] We are about that beauty life! Despite these metrics, Black folk have been largely ignored by global beauty brands. A 2016 survey organised by retail chain Superdrug highlighted that Black women spend an extra £137.52 more on their beauty products per year than any other group.[14] The survey also revealed a whopping 70% of Black British women did not feel that high street stores and brands catered to their needs.[15]

So, what exactly are the consequences of the Black hair and beauty industry not being in the hands of Black people? Sadly, the consequences are pretty dire for our long term health and wellbeing.

In an extensive 2018 environmental study conducted by scholars Jessica S. Helm, Marcia Nishiok, Julia Green Brody and Ruthann Rudel entitled: 'Measurement of endocrine dis-rupting and asthma-associated chemicals in hair products used by black women',[16] they found that hair products marketed to Black women contain high levels of toxic chemicals, which may be linked to illness and diseases. For example, the use of particular hair oils and hair relaxers is associated with higher incidence of fibroids, and increased risk of cancer,[17] with hair products being of particular interest as a potential source of exposure and health disparities.

As we know, certain hair products are more commonly used by Black women, including straightening and moisturising hair products often used to 'assimilate' to white supremacist social beauty norms.[18] Therefore, Black women and children are more likely to use hormone-containing hair and skin products more often than white women and children. With some professional hair straightening products containing and releasing substantial amounts of formaldehyde.

The National Cancer Institute researchers have concluded that, based on data from studies in people and from lab research, exposure to formaldehyde may cause leukaemia, particularly myeloid leukaemia, in humans. To make matters worse, formaldehyde can be found alongside other toxic chemicals such as lye, diethyl phthalate (DEP), nonylphenols, parabens and cyclosiloxanes. These chemicals have traditionally been put in products to improve texture, smell and efficacy—for a long time, they were deemed necessary for the aforementioned outcomes. But new hair care systems and beauty companies have proven otherwise. Providing a safe, effective and Black-owned alternative to the once toxic beauty industry.

In May 2021, the journal *Carcinogenesis* released a study called, 'Hair product use and breast cancer incidence in the Black Women's Health Study'.[19] Some of the evidence in the study found that heavy use of hair relaxers containing lye could be linked to higher risks of oestrogen-receptor-positive breast cancer.[20]

The Journal of Environmental Research revealed that due

to the hair products that Black women use, they are potentially exposed to multiple toxic chemicals that interfere with the body's natural hormones. The study assessed a total of 18 hair products including but not limited to: leave in conditioners, oil treatments, hair relaxers and creams.[21]

Chemicals in hair products generally are unregulated and not rigorously tested to the level they should be specifically as they pertain to health and long term impacts on users.[22]

The Black hair care industry is in need of saving. The products Black women are putting in their hair needs to be safer, healthier and healing. So, who are the entrepreneurs that are working to do just that?

I introduce you to Rachael Corson and Joycelyn Mate, founders of the award winning Afrocenchix. Afrocenchix is an all-natural, vegan and fair trade hair care company which is tailored to the needs of afro hair—without the harmful ingredients. The founding pair 'take incredible care with the marketing and imagery [their] brand promotes and take time to choose models that represent the diversity of afro-hair.' Corson adds that 'all afro curl patterns are equal and need to be represented and seen, as visibility is key' in their line of business. What was most interesting to me, was the way they spoke about invoking a sense of pride in their customers, as for such a long time Black hair has been deemed to be challenging and time consuming.

In the words of Mate herself: 'Looking after Black hair is not labour and it takes the amount of time it takes—we have to unlearn this narrative that looking after ourselves is not worth centring or the time.' When she said that, it felt like a dragging because at the time I was lacklustre with looking after my 4C hair, as I had convinced myself that I did not have the time. I had internalised the white supremacist capitalist machine more than I had realised, to the point that I was not looking after my hair, and myself, in a deserving way.

If you did not know, afro hair has specific needs which often have to be superscribed with customised and tailored care. We need specific targeting shampoos, conditioners, oils and ways to care for our curls. Afrocenchix are providing more than just quality products; they also host regular science and historical based informational talks about afro hair and how to care for it. Their approach is nothing but holistic.

Much like Corson and Mate, Aaron Wallace, the founder of the eponymous Aaron Wallace grooming line, uses great ingredients and the centring of self-care to empower its consumers. The company launched initially in 2016, from inside the Shear and Shine Barbershop in Croydon, South London.

Whilst working as a barber Wallace witnessed the continuing challenges faced by men unable to find quality products that could solve their hair and skincare concerns—so he decided to do something about it. In order to come up with winning formulations, Wallace sat down with his customers on a regular basis to ask them about what they wanted from a product. How they wanted to feel. How they wanted to look.

When we think about the beauty industry, men are often left out of the conversation, as the currency of beauty treatments, by proxy self-care, and feeling good is something that has conventionally been attributed to women because of patriarchal society. But Wallace knew that there was potential to create a product that not only improved a man's appearance but also how he felt about himself. Over the course of two years, Wallace worked alongside experienced formulation experts and manufacturers to develop and test products that would actually work to improve afro hair and skin, without the use of any toxic ingredients.

As part of the Aaron Wallace range you can find potent key ingredients like Black Seed Oil and Mango Butter, which are both rich in nutrients that work to combat dryness, reduce breakage, protect against environmentally caused damage and encourage healthier hair growth.

The founders of Afrocenchix and Aaron Wallace triggered me to think about the ways in which haircare has been a powerful bastion of experience for the Black community, in particular the ways in which salons and barbershops continue to be foundational for the community. Scholar Lawrence Ross describes salons and barbershops as 'sanctuaries away from all things that storm the Black [persons] citadel each day.'[23]

Salons and barbershops have long served as special places among Black folk since the late 19th century providing them with a freedom to create their own success in business whilst serving the needs of their community.[24] But it wasn't always like this, as during the Civil war and early 20th century in America, Black-owned barbershops were frequented mainly by wealthy and upper echelon white men.

This meant that often, Black men were not allowed to visit the stores of their kinfolk for a shave or haircut due to the fact that white men refused to be shaved with the same razor as a Black man.[25] Yup, that's right even in the history of the barbershop, racism rears its ugly head! The need for economic security as well as the understanding the fact that white men were more valued, powerful members of society, meant Black barbers sadly had to oblige[26] to ensure their economic security.[27]

It is also important to note that being a barber was an appealing career path for Black men during that time, as it was less laborious than working on the fields or with animals, which usually involved being exposed to the elements whatever the season.[28]

However, after the emancipation of Slavery, and moving into the 20th Century, salons and barbershops became safe spaces where Black people could be themselves and discuss pertinent issues pertaining to race, culture and politics.[29] They were places to play games such as chess, cards, dominoes and everything in between. Barbershops became and remain Black social and cultural hubs, as shown in films and plays like *Coming to America* (1988), *Malcolm X* (1992), *Barbershop* (2002) and Barber Shop Chronicles (2017).

In 1934, Henry M. Morgan founded the Tyler Barber College in Tyler, Texas, which was then followed by colleges in Houston, Dallas and Little Rock. Morgan was so successful that nearly 80% of all Black barbers in America were trained at one of his schools.[30] At the beginning of the 20th century, barbering brought not only opportunity, but wealth for Black men. Alonzo Herndon, one of the first African-American millionaires, began his empire in 1878 with his first barbershop. Before his death he owned more than 100 rental places, he was the wealthiest Black man in Atlanta.[31] Herndon is often cited as the reason why Atlanta is known for being a centre of Black wealth, Black higher education and Black political power—with his legacy being felt even today.

The history of the Black British barbershop is just as rich and rooted in the same emotional and social historicity of our American counterparts. In the words of Black British journalist Menelik Simpson, the Black British barbershop acts as a 'rite of passage, a place to note the latest hairstyles, slang, learn to debate, mix with other generations, and talk sport, women and politics.'[32] With researcher Larry Walker going further to suggest that without barbershops, Black men would have very few places to feel physically and emotionally safe—making them fundamental for their mental health. Black barbershops in the UK, just like in America, are more than a place to get a haircut and hair salons are more than just a place to get your edges laid. They are places of comfort where Black people can be free without the judgement of the white gaze.

In Black British magazine *Flamingo* (for more on *Flamingo*, see Chapter 3), a short story by Winston Whyte was published in April 1962.[33] The story was titled 'Barber Shop Trial'. In the story Whyte writes about the vibrant and multi-dimensional world of the Black British barbershop. Though fiction, the short story can be read as an anthropological exploration into the societal importance of what Whyte calls 'The Barber Shop Society'.

In one part of the story, Whyte writes about how different his barbershop is from English barbershops, explaining that in English barbershops conversations are not filled with the same depth as his barbershop. Whyte goes on to write that 'any good Jamaican barber is philosopher, preacher, politician, lawyer, father-confessor, comedian and family guidance counsellor all rolled into one.'[34]

Whyte's short story conveys the vital communal functions of these places of business and how they have existed in historic Black British communities for some time. Black-owned Magazine *The Voice* (for more information about *The Voice* see Chapter 3) would distribute adoption surveys in Black hair dressers and Black barbershops for Black customers to read and fill in.[35]

When a young woman named Beryl Gittens, was preparing to leave Guyana for the UK, her uncle suggested she take a pressing comb with her everywhere.[36] She would arrive in the UK in 1952[37] and would open a salon called *Beryl's Hairdressing Salon*[38] in 1962. It would be located on Streatham High Street making it one of the earliest Black-owned hairdressers in London on record.

The 1980s were an active period for Black-owned hair salons and barbers, thanks to the Windrush generation. *Roots*, an upmarket Black-owned hair salon based in Victoria opened in the early 1980s. The hair salon's entrepreneurial spirit would extend further with the founder releasing a magazine, also called *Roots,* that people could get at the hair salon[39]— smart, right?!

Then there were the Mayfair Black-owned hair salons— Splinters and Ebony.[40] The two hair salons were located on Maddox Street, at the centre of Central London and would often compete for customers. Shortly after, in 1986, Cynthia MacDonald opened Back to Eden, a dreadlock hair salon located in New Cross, South London.[41] Rapid developments like these would continue all throughout the 1980s resulting in a Black British Barbershop and Hair Salon boom. The centrality of the Black barbershop and hair salon to the Black British experience has also been reflected in Black British artistic expressions, such as classic sitcom *Desmond's (1989)* and the play Barber Shop Chronicles (2017).

Today, our lifestyles have dramatically changed, there is less time to sit around and wait. Some might argue that we are more busy or, in my opinion, capitalism has commodified time to the point where we feel like we have none. Without getting bogged down into the socio-political discourse of it all, there are some companies that have brilliantly found a bridge between community and time productivity.

Trim-It, founded by Darren Tenkorang and Nathan Maalo, is an Uber-like tech-enabled barber service that allows customers to order a haircut right to their doorstep. The company was able to launch in 2018 after winning £10,000 at a business competition, and since then they have hired a team and powered up more mobile barbering vans to provide their customers with the grooming services they desire.

Trim-It has reimagined the barbershop space and brought it to the modern man. They offer barbering services to all, but the premise of the business shares commonality with Black barbershops across the world. Trim-It provides men with a choice, control over their time, comfort and ability to centre their needs whilst having a great conversation (if they so wish) with fantastic tailored customer service.

Nathan Maalo, co-founder of Trim-It, shared that the business initially started as a marketplace app, where those who were looking for a fresh cut could browse, find barbers in their local area and book it. However, very quickly Maalo and Tenkorang realised that they would have no control over the quality of service. Quality control is something that is missing in the hairdressing industry as the industry is currently unregulated.

There are no general licensing requirements and there is no statutory requirement for hairdressers (including barbers) to hold specified qualifications and the registration of hair-dressing practitioners is voluntary. This was a problem for the duo, as quality was key. In order to shape the barbering industry in the way they wanted, they had to start their own barber shop and bring it into the 21st century to meet the needs of the 21st century consumer.

Similarly, budding entrepreneur Antoinette Ale, has kept accessibility at the centre of her entrepreneurial endeavours. Ale is the founder of Haircrush, a haircare platform for Black women. When asked why she started the company she said, 'I wanted to create a space that would address the gap in British beauty media around Black hair care and celebrate Black women.'

Ale expands on the impetus behind her first hair company, 'I was always around Black hair growing up as I visited my aunt's home salon frequently and this sparked my passion for hair styling. When I started university, I realised I could make extra money from it because there weren't many stylists in the Midlands that did Black hair. Clients would always ask me questions about how they should care for their hair in between appointments. At the time, there wasn't a platform readily sharing information to help Black women build healthy hair routines.'

Ale's next entrepreneurial endeavour will be Tressly, a business she describes as 'a website builder specifically for Black hair stylists. With Tressly, Black hair stylists can easily create a one-page booking site within minutes using templates that are tailored to their business needs.' For Ale, the Black hair space is one the most important for the Black community and ensuring that its development continues to benefit both Black consumers and Black business owners is something she takes seriously.

On how she feels about launching Tressly, she says, 'It's been a long time coming so I'm excited. I've been working on Tressly for over 3 years; doing research, speaking to Black hair stylists, testing our prototype and understanding the pain points. Most importantly, I'm excited for the way it will transform the industry. Tressly is all about economically empowering Black hair stylists and this is just the start of how we want to fulfil that vision.'

It is important to understand that the existence of Black-owned beauty businesses has real added value for Black consumers. When products we put on our body and skin are made by us, the research and due diligence is usually done to ensure they are healthy for us. In such cases it is important to note the difference between a Black-owned company and a company having Black consumers. The latter is the case for many high street brands but having a Black consumer base does not mean that a brand is good for Black skin and hair.

There are a countless amount of brands that are not Black-owned but 'cater' to Black consumers, we also know that quite a few of them are not actually good for us. Black consumers continue to become more educated about what chemicals and ingredients are harmful and healthy for us, so I am hopeful that this increase in consumer consciousness will naturally lead to the support of Black-owned businesses.

Black beauty is rapidly thriving under authentic ownership, whilst being reclaimed, by us for us. Beauty has been and is Black, and I love to see it. Antoinette Ale believes the Black hair care space is one of the most under-reported and underserved segments within the wider beauty industry. 'There is no data that reflects the true size and complexity of it and that still amazes me.' Ale believes 'this presents an opportunity for Black entrepreneurs to take up this space instead of waiting for big conglomerates to finally notice its potential.'

Khalia Ismain is co-founder of Jamii, a Black British discount card with over 25% Black British beauty Businesses on their roster. When it comes to the importance of Black-owned beauty business she explains, 'There's an innate knowledge that comes from Black hair care products being made by businesses that are owned by Black people: they are much more likely to know what's effective, what's healthy and what works for curls and coils.'

For a long time, beauty brands or services have imagined white people as the blueprint customer, and people of colour, Black people more specifically have been an afterthought. The special thing about companies like Afrocenchix, Trim-It and many more, is that they are beauty businesses that are centralising the often ignored Black beauty experience. They are Black owners, who understand and have actually felt the ostracisation of an industry that Black people have, ironically, keep viable through our spending. They reimagine the Black beauty experience and consistently bestow fresh vitality to it.

6

SUSTAINABILITY, ETHICAL CONSUMPTION AND SOCIAL RESPONSIBILITY IN BLACK BRITISH BUSINESSES

One of my favourite past-times is attending startup pitch events.

Let me paint a picture for those who do not know what these events entail. Picture a room, and in this room are budding entrepreneurs, focus groups, investors and almost always a microphone or two. Across the world, almost every day, promising entrepreneurs gather in said rooms in the hope of getting their business idea the valuable exposure it needs. There are, of course, varying degrees to these types of events and importantly there is space for people at varying stages of their entrepreneurial journey.

Some entrepreneurs present with just an idea, a business plan and a minimal viable product (MVP). While others have already launched their services and products to the public, have a rigorous cash flow and understanding of their businesses viability. If you are thinking about starting a business, or just nosily interested in what other people are doing, go to an event—a quick Google search is where I find miscellaneous business events to attend every week. It is a valuable space for everyone involved. These events will awaken your mind to new ideas and get you familiarised with the overused and confusing business jargon.

At an event, one evening, a very enthusiastic, blue-eyed,

20-something, Cambridge grad (he proudly introduced himself as such before even announcing his name) got up and pitched his idea for a fast-fashion menswear line. I, for one, was not expecting him to pitch a fast-fashion company. Most guys with the same profile are usually shouting about how they are going to be the next Uber but 'more out there' (that was literally a response from one entrepreneur), or provide service faster than Deliveroo—often with no explicit ideation on how to do these things.

Their confidence is always predictably audacious. But this guy, who we will call Peter, was unlike any pitcher I had ever seen. He had done his research, cash flow tight, marketing plan superior, and the proposed clothing collection was genuinely trendy. I mean, if I had the £200k lying around that he was asking for, his proposition would have piqued my interest.

The usual structure of these events goes as follows; after each entrepreneur delivers their pitch, the audience and principal investors in the room are invited to ask questions. The aim of these questions are to vet the business further, to discover any gaping or slight holes in the business model.

Commonly asked questions are:

'What is the average percentage markup on each item?'

'How many employees will you have?'

'How did you get to a £2,000,000 evaluation?'

'How much money did you make last quarter?'

'How do you plan to scale the company?'

When I looked around the room after Peter's pitch, everyone was leaning forward, nodding in agreement and jotting down god knows what into their overpriced leather-bound notepads (I am a stationery fiend, so I know an overpriced notepad when I see one). But there was one lady, two rows in front of me, off to the side, dressed in a maroon blazer who politely kept her hand up while Peter confidently answered the investors. I was drawn to her mainly because she kept her hand firmly erect in the air for at least 15 minutes; it did not fall or flinch. The greatest thing about it was that she and Peter had made eye contact, he blinked understandably in her direction as if to signal 'I have seen you, won't forget you—rest b' but despite this, her hand remained in the air.

When it was her time to speak, she spoke in a calm and curious voice. She thanked Peter for his polished pitch, and then after the gushing compliments she proceeded to say, 'but I have a few questions…' which directly translates to 'hold on to your seat because you are about to be dragged.' After attending many of these events, one ends up developing a knack for understanding the true meaning behind other wise politely structured phrases. I live for the phrase *'But I have a few questions…'* when attending pitch events. This is not because I take pleasure in people having their work torn apart, but because what usually follows after 'but I have a few questions…' is of extreme value.

Peter, for the first time in 30 minutes, looked uneasy. The audience sat up in their seats wondering what this maroon blazer lady could possibly have to say against this seemingly perfect pitch. She then proceed to ask him a host of questions, starting with:

'Where do you plan on producing these products?'

'China and Sri Lanka.' Peter answered quickly.

'What is the door to door production turnaround?' She fired back even quicker.

'Roughly 2–4 weeks depending on the product and quantity…' Peters's voice lost confidence with this answer.

I instantly knew where she was going, and I suspect Peter did as well. He stood there, red-faced. She paused for a moment and then delivered the killer question:

'So am I right to assume sustainability, production ethics and anti-slavery measures are not core drivers of your business?'

Just like that, it was over for Peter. The crowd retracted back into their seats, sceptical expressions glazed over their faces. To make matters worse Peter failed to answer the question coherently. His response, frankly, was a train wreck. He stammered through his words and eventually went on to say 'the business world is naturally exploitative and China thrives off of the exploitation of its workforce.'

I sunk into my seat and thought *damn*. Okay Peter, we know that business is driven by capitalism which in its very essence is exploitative. We know some questionable production methods happen in countries where a large part of the economy is driven by the supply and demand needs of the globalised west, but you have got to come better than that! Within seconds, he lost the room. I later found out he did not get the investment he was seeking that evening. I remain convinced that if the maroon blazer lady did not eloquently question him that night, Peter would have got £200k for 10% of his business.

Peter's pitching parable is an excellent example of how ethics can make or break a business or service in today's world. The maroon blazer lady was right to ask those questions because a company's environmental and social impact is under the spotlight in a way that it has never been before.

And as someone who runs a fashion brand myself, I am always looking at the more ethical ways of producing products and how my company can help marginalised groups of people, because firstly it is the right thing to do, but also because it is a growing requirement of customers.

What was most interesting is that all of the investors that evening were most definitely boomers and generation X, while the maroon blazer lady was a millennial on the cusp of Generation Z like myself.[1] Millennials are more likely to support a business, brand, cause and people that they connect with emotionally. Data-driven marketing company *Epsilon* found that social impact and social media are extremely important to Millennials in their buying journey because even though they value the opinions of family and friends, they actively want to know where their products come from.[2]

In addition to this, according to Synchrony, 82% of millennials would agree that social and political topics of discussion are a key influencer when it comes to purchasing.[3] With Gen Z sharing a similar psychology, however, they are more selective when making big expenditures, with many often buying products only when they're on sale or even delaying gratification by waiting for newer products to become available.[4]

In 2020, the year of the Black Lives Matter Movement, we saw the ways in which Black Twitter drove the charge to expose companies for their non inclusive practices. Whether that be their treatment of employees, their policies or the ways in which they use Blackness for profit but shun Black consumers when in store by following them around like petty thieves.

Companies were forced to be transparent regarding the diversity of the companies. A person who led this charge was Sharon Chuter, founder of UOMA Beauty. Chuter was born in Nigeria, but she was raised in London, and has a long career in beauty, before becoming an entrepreneur she worked as an executive at the LVMH group. She launched the 'Pull Up or Shut Up' campaign as a means to call out organisations for their internal diversity and inclusion leadership representation.

Chuter urged the public to do their own research about each brand and to reconsider where they were putting their investments through buying products. If we value sustainability, ethics, diversity and inclusion, surely we should be buying from companies that present that it is important to them behind the scenes in who they hire, promote and have at the senior table? The hashtag #PullUpOrShutup has been embraced by influencers such as YouTuber Jackie Aina, with companies like E.L.F. Cosmetics, Milk Makeup, Versed and Cover FX offering up their diversity and inclusion stats and making open pledges to work on those metrics.

When we think about sustainability, we are always drawn to think about our impact on people and the environment, but forget about how important that element of diversity and inclusion is. People more than ever, want to know about who is producing and is behind the clothes they wear, programmes they watch and services they use. In my line of work as a Director of Diversity and Inclusion, people always ask me things like: 'Why is diversity so important if business has existed until this point without it?'

My short answer is that if you want to run a sustainable business, and by that I mean survive as a company, financially and also with a succession of people who want to work for you, you must consider what the infrastructure of your business looks like because that is what is being required by Millennials and Gen Z—the people who hold the future purse strings.

If we think back to Peter's fast-fashion brand, where he was targeting mainly Gen Z, with the promise of cheap, on-trend, designer style replicas, which image-led Gen Z crave. We can see where Peter fell short. I mean, he was not totally wrong, Gen Z do love a designer replica but the move towards sustainability, social responsibility and these poignant conversations about the future of the planet meddle in the minds of these two generations.

Against all the profit being made, Millennials and Gen Z are more concerned about the future, sustainability and ethics than their fore folk. Despite the continual pop-up of ultra-successful fast-fashion brands that never seem to make it past the three-year viability test: millennials and Gen Z are more socially and politically aware, hyper-conscious and concerned about almost everything.

These two younger generations bring topics to light to the older generations, just as the maroon jacket lady did that evening to the investors. Now, I can look back and see that it was the adrenaline of pent up resistance and the need to spread the importance of social responsibility and ethics that kept that maroon lady's hand so strong that evening.

In 2013, the eight story Rana Plaza factory collapsed on the outskirts of Dhaka, Bangladesh. To date, this is one of the worst factory catastrophes of the 21st century, more than 1,200 people were killed with a further 2,500 seriously hurt, leaving many with debilitating life changing injuries. These workers were paid a pittance, roughly 2,500 Bangladeshi Taka a month, which converts to roughly £23. There is no other way to describe that wage other than disgustingly exploitative.

These workers were paid a pittance, in exchange for 16 hours of work a day and ultimately their lives. Children and women close to their due dates of birth were found amongst the rubble, alongside the tags of retailers such as Mango, Primark and H&M. As with every disaster, many of the companies released statements, condolences and admitted that they needed to do more to protect its 'most valuable' workers on the bottom of the pyramid. But as expected, not much has changed.

In July 2020, fast fashion brand BooHoo, which targets both Gen Z and millennial buyers (16-40) and is the mother company to brands such as Nasty Gal and 'we all have the same 24-hours' Pretty Little Thing, found itself in the midst of controversy after a undercover Sunday Times investigation exposed that the fashion giant was paying workers as little as £3.50 an hour, less than half the legal minimum wage, in various factories around Leicester, England.[5]

This uncovering saw the fashion brand dropped from the websites of fellow fashion retailers Next, ASOS and Zalando, which within two days haemorrhaged over £1,500,000,000 of its £5,000,000,000 open evaluation. To add insult to injury, the workers' rights group 'Labour Behind the Label' claimed employees at factories that supplied to the three fast fashion companies were being forced to come into work while sick with COVID-19. Yes, you read that correctly.

Often when we think of poor working conditions, pay and treatment, we reserve it for Asian countries where labour laws are lax, where the factories main aim is to supply as quickly as possible for our ridiculous, and selfish demands in the globalised west. For a long time, people did not think about where their clothes came from, all they thought of was, 'where can I get a t-shirt for £4?' or 'OMG, this dress is £1.'

Not one moment was spent thinking about where it was made, who made it, or for what price. No one stopped to think that even when selling a dress for £1 the company was still making a profit, so how much were the workers being paid? Probably less than the 76p the workers of the Rana Plaza factory were being paid per day. But as noted before, this issue is not only reserved for Asian countries, it happened here on our 'own soil' too. I cannot help but suspect that Next, ASOS and Zalando's response was due to the BooHoo exposé happening so close to home, which made it less okay from a PR perspective.

This is linked to race undoubtedly, as a society we have been prepped to think about exploitation outside of the context of the United Kingdom. Exploitation is foreign, that is the business of countries like China and India. They are the ones who force workers to do 20 hour shifts in poor conditions, England could never do a thing such as that! But I ask, who are these countries making products for? Yeah, the UK and other countries in the globalised west. We have known about the poor conditions of these factories for years now, but it happening on Britain's front door was a step too far.

To name but a few, Peter's pitching parable and BooHoo demonstrate why contemporary businesses need to do more to ensure that they are centring factors other than profits into their success. It would seem being socially responsible and ethical are key factors in ensuring a businesses survival in today's economy.

Sustainability in the business world is when a business attempts to create long-term business value by considering how its business operates in relation to the ecological, social and economic environment.

Businesses have not always sought to be sustainable and some still don't. However, thanks to the millennial and Gen Z generation, consumers now want sustainable businesses. Due to this trend, being a sustainable business often comes with brand enhancement that attracts and keeps customers as well as attracting an innovative workforce. In 2019, HSBC released their 'Made for the Future' report. It revealed that almost half of UK companies planned to increase their environment-related spending between 2019 and 2021.[6]

In 2020 Accenture's global survey revealed that consumerism changed hugely during the pandemic, highlighting that 60% of consumers reported purchasing products and services that were more sustainable, environmentally friendly and/ethical purchases.[7] The survey also showed that 90% of consumers said that they would continue to purchase products and services in this way. So, sustainable businesses are in and according to the data this is likely something that will be sticking around.[8] So where does that leave the relationship between Black British businesses and sustainability?

In many cases, there is a financial cost of being a sustainable business. Businesses are motivated, for the most part, by profit and sustainability is looked at as expensive. In an article titled, 'Why more than half of UK businesses are planning to increase spend on sustainability' published in the *Telegraph*,[9] the sustainability manager of Innocent drinks admits sustainability is more expensive but due to their company ethos, their company chooses to commit to the sustainability route.

One entrepreneur willing to foot the cost is Nina Hopkins the founder of sustainable fashion brand Jakke. Hopkins has been able to bridge the gap between profits and ethics by ensuring that they consistently re-evaluate where they source their materials, how their clothes are made and the impact their existence as a business has on society. Over 40% of their online collection is made from recycled plastic, and through their work in the community, they equip the next generation with knowledge of how to confidently buy into ethical fashion.

Having to pay more to produce your product or service is, of course, an easier burden to bear for larger businesses. Sustainability investments within a business usually offer very long term results and in many cases the results are intangible.

For many businesses, a lot of time is taken up by managing the short term impacts on the bottom line and leads to intangible results as opposed to short term effects on the bottom line.[10]

So, when we look at what kind of businesses can afford to look at and prioritise long term and intangible results in the name of sustainability, we see it tends to be those who quite literally can *afford* it.[11] As we have explored, Black-owned businesses already face huge barriers to entry including a lack of access, being underfunded and under supported thus we can deduce that for the average Black-owned business, being sustainable may be a luxury they cannot afford.

However, for those whose product or service itself is not rooted in producing or providing a sustainable good or item, being sustainable may not always be accessible even if founders want this to be the case.

This is of course not to say there are not Black-owned sustainable businesses because there certainly are—some Black British ones include:

AKOJO MARKET

AKOJO MARKET is a platform that sells handmade accessories, jewellery, homeware and fashion from independent African designers, who are committed to artisan craftsmanship and sustainable and transparent ways of working.

YAKO BEAUTY

Yako Beauty is a London based hair care brand delivering a range of products made from natural plant and fruit extracts. Their hair care products are created for a variety of hair types, and come in sustainable packaging and recyclable tubes.

LYNCH & MASON

Lynch & Mason is a luxury menswear tailoring brand specifically designed for tall self-identifying men that uses ethically sources luxury fabrics.

ATIJO STORE

Atijọ Store offers customers a collection of exclusively curated vintage designer and unique products, with the mission to bring new light to the landscape of pre-loved clothing and encourage slow and conscious buying while celebrating timeless style, diversity and culture.

Social responsibility is an ethical theory that argues that individuals are responsible for civic duties. Social responsibility in business or corporate social responsibility (CSR), as it is commonly referred to, takes this theory and applies it to the business world. CSR asserts that businesses have a duty to act in the interests of their wider society. The crux of this idea is ethical balance, allowing businesses to commit to profitability as well as the welfare of others. When ascribing to social responsibility theory, a business must employ the societal goals of a philanthropic activity, activism, or be of a charitable nature by engaging in or supporting ethically oriented practices. Whilst this shares some similarities and crossover with the idea of sustainability in businesses, the two are different.

The Co-Op 'Ethical Consumer UK Market Report' has tracked UK ethical expenditure since 1989.[12] In 2014, the report revealed that growth in the value of ethical spending between 2012 and 2013 was 9%, and by the time of the survey was worth £32,200,000,000. The report also highlighted that, '20 percent of the UK population is now actively boycotting specific products or retail outlets as a result of their ethical concerns.'[13] The 2020 update of the same report showed that by the end of 2019, 'ethical consumer spending and finance in the UK reached £98 billion.'[14] It also revealed that British consumers were actively reducing energy consumption, shopping locally and purchasing Fair Trade items more.[15]

William Adoasi, CEO and designer of Vitae London watches, has managed to find the equilibrium between profit and social ethics, which makes the brand inherently socially responsible. Adoasi, born south of the river, and reared in Camberwell and Peckham, but of Ghanaian heritage is a true trailblazer, as he is the first young Black person in the UK to own a watch company on the scale that he does and raise money like he has. In doing so he has gained recognition from celebrities such as Sir Richard Branson for his contributions to the fashion industry.

Through doing this he has shown that 'Black people have more to offer,' other than just rapping about and wearing timepieces—we now own them and in doing so are making a difference to grassroots communities. Luxury timepieces are no longer reserved for well-to-do, middle class, aged white men, as Vitae watches also come without the whopping price tag. Adoasi explains that he had a social responsibility not to 'price customers out of being able to give back to the global community,' which is why the Vitae watches are affordable.

Adoasi has been able to flip the industry on its head, and subvert the watch from a symbol of wealth to one of giving back to others. When you wear one of the Vitae watches, you have made a difference in the world. Adoasi has been able to secure numerous partnerships which have helped further the brand's mission to help Sub-Saharan Africa children access the bare necessities which in England are often commoditised.

Vitae is in partnership with the South African based

non-profit House of Wells, which 'exists to restore hope, dignity and release the potential of children and youth in Africa,' and is helping bring light to young people's lives with the alliance of Pen To Paper Ghana, a non-governmental organisation that aims to improve education and facilities for the youth of Ghana.

Through this partnership Vitae is able to provide children across Sub-Saharan Africa with a solar powered LED light (10 hours of power per charge), as a lack of electricity poses a threat to educational advancement. Children often have to burn kerosene and other harmful fuels to get light, or as Adoasi shares from his more recent trips to Ghana, ' kids would often walk for miles to the nearest street lamp to complete their studies in the evenings, but now, through [his business he] gets to be the solution.' In the words of Adoasi, 'it takes a village to 'watch' the next generation.'

In Ghana, school is often free and on children's doorsteps, but it is the additional costs that prevent them from accessing their right to education. That is why with each timepiece Vitae equips a child with two sets of uniform, without these uniforms they would be turned away from school. From the very start of the Vitae journey, Adoasi was determined to incorporate a social element into his business model. He shared with me that his father was the first person in his family to learn to read and write and would talk about the unnecessary barriers that stopped his peers from getting an education. These stories proved to be a great insight for Adoasi, as he was able to 'pin-point what we needed to give back in a purposefully meaningful way.'

When it comes to the balance between profitability and social responsibility, today, in some cases, social responsibility has become a large part of business models. This is because of the increase in 'ethical consumerism'. Ethical consumerism is when consumers purchase from and support businesses that produce products and services that result in minimal environmental and/social harm. While avoiding products and services deemed to have a negative impact on society or the environment. These businesses are structured around being socially responsible, as for them profitability = social responsibility. Can ethical consumerism and corporate social responsibility boost Black-owned businesses?

What occurred in the business world after the brutal killing of George Floyd in 2020 was unprecedented. Very quickly, we saw 'the ethical consumer' decide to spend their money on Black Owned businesses or businesses who were supporting the wider Black community through charitable means, economically and other ways. Hashtags such as #SupportBlackBusinesses began to trend and all eyes were on Black-owned businesses, both big and small.[16]

Many Black businesses (both British and American) saw an increase in profit and sales that they had never seen before. In the case of Black-owned businesses, the sudden rush to purchase from them in some instances resulted in owners being overwhelmed.[17] For many, the increase in profits meant Black-owned companies were able to take advantage of the interest in Black-owned businesses using the capital to expand teams, or re-invest in their companies.[18]

For the most part this development, at least on the surface appears positive. However, when considering that the wider initiative to support Black-owned businesses was the result of the brutal murder of a Black man—is this really a good thing? What does it say about the average consumer if we were led to support Black businesses only in the instance of Black trauma?

A report from crowd-sourced local business review and social networking site Yelp showed that between May and July of 2020 there were over 2,500,000 searches for Black-owned businesses and Black authors, compared to approximately 35,000 over the same time period the previous year which is a 7,043% increase.[19]

In 2020 Jamii and Translate culture produced their 'Black Lives Matter & Black Pound Day Consumer Report'. The report assessed the impact of the BLM movement on Black British businesses. The report revealed the increase in spending within Black-owned businesses and, interestingly, the increase and power of ally purchasing power.

I believe that the data trend might be a reflection of our natural psychological reaction to pain as human beings combined with our push to be led by what everyone else is doing. Something tragic happens, we see everyone is reacting and we follow suit. Now monetarily speaking, the injection of money to Black-owned businesses via this route can be beneficial insofar as businesses get access to cash flow they haven't had access to and this can assist in the short term and in some cases provide money for long term investment. However, it also provides a set of problems, as this kind of money injection is very rarely sustainable—quite simply, it might not last.

There is a term that became increasingly used after the aftermath of the resurgence of the 2020 Black Lives Matter movement—performative activism. Performative activism is allyship and activism that is enacted with the aim of inflating one's social value rather than genuine care about the social cause.

I would be able to buy myself 10 boxes of plantain in Dalston Market for the amount of times white people at work smiled with glee as they showed me their new tea towels, furniture, books and jewellery that they bought from a Black-owned business.

The question always remains, when the moment passes (because it will), how are Black entrepreneurs meant to ensure their businesses remain supported by consumers?

Active allyship is a consistent and ongoing practice of unlearning and relearning, where those in a position of privilege seek to be in solidarity with the group they are supporting. That would mean consciously and truly supporting Black-owned businesses and showing up outside of the tragic events and certain times of the year like Black History Month and Blackout Days*. Active Allyship requires an acknowledgement that to ensure the sustainability and longevity of Black-owned businesses and economic empowerment you will have to spend money with them.

Also, in this active allyship, one should acquaint themselves with the different sociological reasons for the reason why Black businesses are not supported or start out with less social equity than their white counterparts. For example, there have been generational barriers to Black families starting businesses, meaning that Black parents have gone into more stable and traditional careers and jobs.

Sociological studies have found that children that had a self-employed parent are roughly two to three times as likely to be self-employed as someone who did not have a self-employed parent, demonstrating the strong intergenerational link which limits business ownership opportunities for Black people.[20] Understanding these historical and social factors must be the foundation to why people should stand in allyship with Black-owned businesses.

---

* #BlackoutDay aims to unite Black people in economic solidarity through a campaign encouraging participants to support Black-owned businesses exclusively.

7

SEEDS AND MONEY TREES: INVESTMENT FOR BLACK BRITISH BUSINESSES

When things get hard in business, I always find myself randomly shouting 'me and my n****s tryna get it, ya bish' from Kendrick Lamar's 2012 song 'Money Trees.' After shouting the lyrics out and usually being told off by my mother for screaming profanity in her house, I wonder why those words are drawn from the deepest crevice of my unconscious. Every time it leaves my lips, it is as if I am repelling and rejecting something. Some days 'ya bish' is HMRC, or a Santander text message telling me to add cash to the business account before 2pm so that payments can clear. Sometimes 'ya bish' is the company website crashing before a collection drop. But oftentimes, 'ya bish' is used to embody the white supremacist patriarchal systems that quite frankly stand in the way of me and n****s getting it!

Entrepreneurs have it hard, and Black entrepreneurs have it harder. Black start-up founders typically have higher education levels and more lived corporate experience before starting their business than their white counterparts. Despite this, the British Business Bank found that Black businesses report a median turnover of £25,000 per year which is a third less than white business owned businesses.[1] Additionally, the bank found that 28% of Black business owners fail to make a profit compared to 16% for white business owners, and even fewer meet their business aspirations.[2]

Just 30% of Black entrepreneurs say they met their financial aims and only half met their non-financial goals.[3] This compares unfavourably to white business owners, where over 54% say their business met economic-based aims and 69% met their non-financial goals.[4] They also found that Black and Asian founders invested more time and bootstrapped money when developing their business ideas than white entrepreneurs.

The British Business Bank concluded that these disparities were caused by 'a host of interconnected and systemic factors,'[5] also known as, 'ya bish' white supremacist patriarchal structures, which include things like: the inability to access finance, social capital, generational household income deprivation and the presence of un-diverse directors and officials in the workplace, which reduces the opportunity to develop business-relevant skills, knowledge and networks.

I remember where I was and what I was wearing when I first heard about a 'friend and family round'. I was on a board with some provocative, disruptive founders who had changed the face of retail, fintech and marketing. I was gassed[6] to be there but on the very first meeting, all the entrepreneurs were asked to say a little something about themselves and how they were able to get their business off the ground.

Mr Fintech shared that after leaving Cambridge University, his parents and distant relatives gave him more than £50,000 to get started and shared that he never thought about being an entrepreneur until his private school had accountants and business owners come in to speak to them about the ins and outs of it.

Señorita Retail shared the difficulties of being a female founder and why she wants little girls who look like her from small places like Oxford—I am guessing those girls have long cascading blonde hair and live in detached houses with lots of fresh air—to know that they too can start a million-pound business out of their parents converted garage.

Then there was me, Tskenya, who had to share that I was still working on my successes and explain that I had no garage and no friends or family who could financially support me. Mr Fintech looked down at his iPad in quiet guilt, Señorita Retail gave me a gentle smile, it was then that I realised I was there to provide variety, colour and the buzzword of the year, *diversity*. I was there so that when people read the reports and suggestions released by this group and questioned how such a privileged group of people could know what marginalised young entre-preneurs needed, they could point to me. Yup, that's right, I was the token Black girl.

That day I learnt that money is and will continue to be a barrier to entry for non-white entrepreneurs. It doesn't matter how hard you hustle, or how early you get up to grind—money and resources will prove to be an issue the more intersections there are to your identity. 'The Black Report 2020', the first qualitative report on Black startup founders in the UK, found that 88% of Black founders self-fund their startups commit-ting an average of £14k from full-time work and side hustles to pump money into their businesses, with 22% of founders being able to raise a family and friends round to kick start their business idea. We also know that many entrepreneurs from minority communities end up taking out personal loans to get their business started as opposed to the usual business loans.[7]

The timeless proverb goes, 'Men lie, women lie but numbers never lie'. Over the course of this book and this chapter so far, we have looked at statistics, surveys, studies because data matters. One area that gives us a good insight to how racial inequality impacts our financial mobility is a quick look at household incomes.

In the UK, white households have incomes 63% higher

than Black households. According to The Office for National Statistics, even after taxes and benefits they are nearly a fifth better off.[8] The average white household income in the financial year to 2019 was £42,371, compared with £35,526 in Asian households and £25,982 in African-Caribbean households.[9] After tax and benefits, the average white household had a 'final' income of £38,222, 9% more than Asians on £35,023, and 18% more than Black households on £32,353.[10]

So what does this actually mean? It means Black people have significantly less startup capital than their non-Black peers. They are less likely to have extra cash to bootstrap their business, raise a friends and family round of investment or have property to leverage. These are just some of the barriers Black people encounter when trying to attain the capital they need to either start a business or develop an already existing business.

FRONTIERS TO INVESTMENT FOR BLACK BUSINESSES

'Is there *really* a big enough market?'

Tobi Oredein, founder of Black Ballad, has heard this question many times. Sadly, it is a question that almost all Black entrepreneurs who cater to their community have heard.

When it comes to investing in any company, there is one foundational sentiment that is at the core of the process—*understanding*. It may sound simple, but its importance cannot be underestimated.

'INVESTMENT IS VERY PERSONAL, IF PEOPLE CAN'T CONNECT WITH YOUR BUSINESS, THEY DON'T WANT TO KNOW.' —TOBI OREDEIN

Tobi Oredein touches on the crucial point of investors understanding the Black market. When it comes to Black Ballad, Tobi Oredein admits the investors that have invested into her company at the time of our interview are predominantly Black (bar one South Asian woman).

Why? Because they get it. It is that simple. When an investor understands your market, you as a founder, your product and your community—they are more likely to give you a shot.

Tobi Oredein speaks to how she and her co-founder knew that as Black entrepreneurs they could never go to an investor meeting with just a business plan, even though their white counterparts were, unfairly, able to and still get the investment they needed. This is the burden of being a Black person in business in the investor world—you are not given the opportunity to fail in the way that others are.

Oredein speaks about how being a Black entrepreneur is very much a do or die thing, because you only have yourself. There is no bank of mum and dad, no rich friend or network to lend you some capital.

Like many young Black British entrepreneurs, Liv Little, founder of the award winning magazine gal-dem, wasn't educated on the investment world. In our conversation for the book, she reflects on the difficulty of being an entrepreneur, 'running a business is stressful and we don't talk about those parts of it enough.'

As a founder when you are trying to attain investment it

is even more challenging. Little was working full time at gal-dem, so trying to get to grips with the investment world was practically impossible, but she knew it was something she needed to understand. She decided to go freelance for a year so she could spend her year learning the ins and outs of the investment world. It was a new world for her. The year would be filled with learning, preparing and building relationships and then three months actually trying to get investment. Liv describes the experience as 'intense and emotionally draining,' acknowledging that 'when you meet the right people and they get it, it's great, but it's not easy.'

More often than not Black British entrepreneurs do not meet the *right* people in investment. Because the investment industry is not diverse and so you often find yourself pitching to people who cannot see the current and future value of you or your market.

Both Tobi Oredein and Liv Little have carved out vital spaces for Black voices in the media landscape, daring to take a leap and in turn providing opportunities for so many women who look just like them. On the topic of investment for Black British business—Tobi Oredein relays a sentiment that applies to almost all areas of Black British entrepreneurship, 'we have a long way to go.'

Khalia Ismain, co-founder of Black British marketplace Jamii, notes that when it comes to capital and Black British businesses, there can be a variety of challenges and many routes lead to knowledge gaps and lack of access to information. Ismain highlights a statistic that has been widely discussed over the last 2 years, that less than 1% of investment in the UK ends up in Black-owned businesses. Ismain states that this 'results from two overarching issues: a lack of access to education on the various forms of funding and what it takes to attain them and a disconnect between the Black business owners and the decision makers.' Ismain continues, stating that the miseducation or lack of education when it comes to investment often leads to 'the pursuit of inappropriate types of finance—or sometimes, leading to businesses not having the confidence to look for funding at all.'

When it comes to getting in the field and attempting to obtain funding for a Black British business, Ismain touches on a similar point to that of Little and Oredein, 'the issue is often that the people making the decisions on whether or not a business should get funding—be it a loan or equity investment—often don't understand or adequately respect the markets being addressed, nor do they see sufficient potential in the entrepreneur in front of them.'

The funding challenges that Black British entrepreneurs face has recently led to Black British entrepreneurs crossing the pond to the USA in search of potential investment opportunities.[11] This shift reveals a growing trend of Black British business attaining a growing level of success in garnering the necessary funds abroad as opposed to on their home turf.

Black on Black financial support is not a new concept in the wider Black community. The concept of 'money pools' has existed for a long time. It is in fact an ancient African tradition, historically used to aid families and individuals in areas of survival, domestic costs and business.[12] This tradition is believed to have existed before the formal concept of 'a bank'.[13]

Money pools in the Black community are informal and communal, where groups, often family and friends, lend and save money for each other. The collectively saved money often goes around the family landing with an individual before the process begins again. These financial collectives often served radical purposes, helping Black people maintain or succeed during colonial times and even slavery.[14] Today, money pools in Black homes continue and have different names depending on where your place of origin is.

One example of this is the company Lendoe, founded by entrepreneur Demi Ariyo. Lendoe is a finance company dedicated to Black, ethnic minority, early stage and women led businesses. In Ariyo's own words, the ethos of Lendoe is, 'to solve the access problem—particularly the *access to finance* issue.' Ariyo explains, 'our viewpoint is that all entrepreneurs should have access to the tools they need to thrive, based on their ability. Not their colour, gender, community or background—so we support these underestimated entrepreneurs, particularly those from Black and Brown backgrounds.'

Ariyo states the biggest challenges for Black British entrepreneurs when it comes to capital and funding is 'access'. He explains this is 'not only access to capital but networks and opportunities.'

On the topic of Black entrepreneurs raising capital, Ariyo notes that there are many ways to raise capital but highlights that Black entrepreneurs often focus on two routes 'Venture Capital—a form of funding given to a select few in return for a share of one's business—and Term Loans—a form of funding given in return for the principal amount given plus interest over a period of time.' Ariyo tells us that 'both of these forms of capital fall under Equity & Credit, however, within Equity and Credit there are several other forms of finance such as invoice finance, purchase order finance, grants, crowdfunding, family and friend money and much more.'

Companies like Lendoe are hugely important, they provide access, financial assistance and information in an area that is often murky and challenging for Black entrepreneurs. They also are an important avenue for proving the viability of Black businesses in an industry that often does the opposite. When asked about why Lendoe is indeed important, Ariyo states, 'Representation. We started in the Black community and will always have a special bond with entrepreneurs from these communities.'

Ariyo explains, 'By doing so, and displaying the success of the Black entrepreneurs we've backed and supported, our customers give the next generation of Black and under-valued entrepreneurs who may experience similar disparities to Black entrepreneurs the hope they need to either continue in entre-preneurship or get started. Knowing that there are companies out there who value them and are willing to support them in achieving their dreams.'

On the matter of what can be done and what needs to change in the future, Ariyo goes back to the word 'access'. He expands further, saying that what is specifically needed is 'access firstly, to information, then to networks and that should be other entrepreneurs and funders who offer the different funding forms or have raised funding and lastly opportunities.'

DEMI ARIYO'S MONEY TIPS FOR BLACK BRITISH ENTREPRENEURS

1. START WITH THE END IN MIND:
More often than not, the money you raise has a lot to do with your end goal. If you are going to build a £100,000,000 business, there's a type of money you are going to need today to ensure you can put the necessary infrastructure in place to get there—Usually venture capital. If you are going to build a £10,000,000 business then it's

likely you'll need a different type of capital, i.e. angel funding and bank financing. It's all about getting a clear understanding of the end goal.

2. GET IN THE RIGHT NETWORKS:

There are networks out there that have special access because of relationships, experience and the knowledge that people within these networks already have. Tapping into such networks will save you time and resources.

3. FOCUS ON BUILDING VALUE:

Raising money is important but ultimately it's about building a business that solves a problem and adds value. As long as you do that, you'll find the money because money follows value. So out of everything I'd say focus on this more than anything else.

Andy Davis was 25 years old when he started 10x10 with his co-founders. The 10x10 group was founded to help invest in Black founders, helping break down those barriers that Black founders are faced with. Before starting 10x10 Andy had built numerous teams, founded start-ups, acquired customers, and raised external capital, so after all of that experience he felt he had the relevant experience to be able to share learnings and support other Black founders.

His mission with the 10x10 fund was to support Black founders in the early stage of business and give them the support required to get to that next stage; plus, to empower the wider Black community to become interested in investment and venture capital. Andy wanted to create a fund where Black founders could develop their ideas in the safe surrounding of Black venture capitalists who understand those socio-economics barriers that impede Black entrepreneurs from succeeding. The 10x10 fund wants to fast-forward Black culture by supporting the exceptional ideas Black founders have.

The 10x10 fund does not just support Black founders with venture capital, but with every aspect of their business evolution, from fundraising to hiring, people management, product, operations, and most importantly customers, the fund is there to facilitate founders to tap into great success outside of their immediate network.

We are very aware of the frontiers facing Black founders, but Davis argues that we must still beat against the current and 'do the work', trust your vision and stick by it, as in his experience investors want to invest in the best businesses and not people-pleasers. Investors want people who have the gusto to take the plunge. It goes without saying that Black founders have more hoops to jump through but having 'world-dominating ambition' will naturally communicate to investors the fruits of your labour as a Black entrepreneur and boost the propensity to invest in the business.

Davis believes that the future of Black business and the way we will capture investors will be beyond anything we can dream. But he urges that we must continue to build on our knowledge, business acumen and cultural competency and continue to develop our networks on a global scale.

It is a secret expectation of many venture capital funds that entrepreneurs raise friends and family rounds. I challenge that this expectation is born of bias and unconscious discrimination due to a lack of socio-economic, historical understanding. In the UK, according to the Office of National Statistics, white British households were approximately nine times as likely to be in the top quintile of total wealth (wealth above £865,400) than those of Black African or Caribbean ethnicity.[15] Meaning that with this lack of access to early capital and generational wealth, most family members and friends can not invest, regardless of how great the idea is.

In general, banking institutions are failing Black people and Black entrepreneurs. The Black Business Network was sponsored by Lloyds Bank to explore the perceptions that Black entrepreneurs have of the banking sector, with the report exposing that only 43% of Black entrepreneurs believe that banks have their best interests in mind. The report surveyed more than 800 Black British people, and starkly outlined not only the severe lack of trust in banks, but also that only 27% of Black people believed the national government had their best interests in mind.[16]

Respondents stated that they would be less likely to approach banks or financial institutions due to their legacy of systemic racism towards ethnic minority folk, which is also compounded by Black business owners' experiences of negative societal discrimination.[17]

This legacy has impacted Black entrepreneurs' propensity to want to borrow from big banks, making their businesses more likely to be bootstrapped. Historically, borrowing money from banks has been the traditional way that entrepreneurs have expanded and grown their businesses. Black businesses opting out of this option means that they are not only missing out on support from traditional lenders, but also the resources banks offer to entrepreneurs by way of mentoring and business networking.

Nigerian born but Britain based Tosin Akinluyi is a Managing Director of Morgan Stanley. Akinluyi was the first Black person, more specifically Black woman, to serve on Morgan Stanley's EMEA Operating Committee. Her experiences as a Black woman in an industry that has been predominantly dominated by white men, as well as her awareness of the Black community's distrust in traditional banking and investment, is part of the reason why she has dedicated the last 20 years of her career to bank advocacy. Akinluyi consistently talks about the value of diversity, inclusion and financial legacy whilst going out into communities to impart her knowledge with business owners and women about the value of not only investing yourself but also in your ideas and businesses.

In 2012, Morgan Stanley launched their Multicultural Innovation Lab in the United States to support companies founded by women and ethnic minorities. In 2021, they expanded the fintech programme to support start-up founders in London, UK. Morgan Stanley are tackling the diversity investment gap in the UK head on, as over the past decade less than 3% of venture capital funds went to woman founders, and less than 2% to teams made up of ethnic minority founders, demonstrating the multi-faceted, systematic barriers Black businesses face when securing financing. Overall, Black entrepreneurs have the least access to capital and between 2009 and 2019 just 0.24% of venture capital went to teams of Black entrepreneurs—around 38 businesses in total. Out of those, only one Black female founder raised Series A funding during that time.

In the United States, the program has supported about 50 startups since 2017 and has raised over $80,000,000 in additional funding since the completion of the Morgan Stanley Accelerator Program,[18] and Morgan Stanley are confident they can match those figures here in the UK.[19]

SO WHERE DO WE GO FROM HERE?

Black entrepreneurs are frequently rejected by investors, some well known cases include Black British entrepreneur Pat McGrath, Richelieu Dennis, (founder of Shea Moisture), Cathy Hughes and the list really does go on.[20]

The search for capital and funding is part of any entrepreneurial journey, but as we have seen it is even harder for Black entrepreneurs to take part in this crucial facet of business building. So what can be done? Well, we can promote and buy from those businesses. Do not be cheap and ask for discounts, or slate the price of a product or service. If you cannot afford it, do not worry your pretty head, it is a free market, spend within your means and leave that Black business alone. At the end of the day, investors will want to see the numbers and have demonstrations of social impact so let's give to those businesses when they deserve it.

When putting your business forward for investment, make sure your deck (business plan) is clear, concise and hones in on your niche, should you have one. Talk about your personal attributes, experience and what you bring to the table— believe in your sauce. Having a great idea is not enough if you're a person of colour in business, well, at least for now it is not. Explain how your idea will solve a problem, and do not worry if your idea is not unique, *you* are what makes it worth investing in.

Practise your pitch. In front of the mirror, your partner, your family, friends, your pet dog. The more you practise talking about your business, the more you will grow in confidence in articulating why your business idea is viable. People invest in other people, so if you carry yourself with confidence that will translate to your investors no doubt! Self-confidence is a journey, you will have good days and bad days, but practice makes perfect.

Finally, do not be afraid of the word no. This business ting is not for the faint hearted and you are going to have to become robust in the face of critique. Not everyone will believe in your vision, and that is okay. You just keep working on that vision and bussin' down doors, you will get your yes and there will be a guiding light. Just be patient, what is for you will be for you.

8

THE COLOUR OF COVID AND DRIVING CHANGE

I began writing this chapter in the midst of the COVID-19 pandemic. Shops were stripped bare due to anxiety-induced stockpiling, toilet paper, hand sanitiser, paracetamol and Heinz baked beans had been scarce for weeks. It was a challenging time to say the least, eye-opening and in many ways felt dystopian. The pandemic caused major societal changes, some temporary, some permanent. Whilst our government was in the full swing of partygate, for the rest of us, COVID-19 disrupted everyday life as we knew it—from holidays, weddings, funerals, schooling, work styles, graduations, family reunions and so much more.

As a global family, we are yet to weigh up the true scale and devastating effects of coronavirus on communities, businesses and the economy. In Britain alone, 21,000 more companies had collapsed by the end of March 2020 versus the year before, and startups fell by roughly 23%[1], which gave economists a clear indication as to where the pandemic would lead us—into another economic recession.

Experts will declare a recession when a country's economy experiences a negative domestic product (GDP), falling sales across varying categories, widespread layoffs, rising levels of unemployment and the decline of income from sectors such as manufacturing. Despite recessions being considered an inevitable part of any economy, by August 2020 British economists declared that we had entered the deepest recession since records began. The pandemic sent the economy plunging by 20.4% between April and June—with no signs of recovering quickly due to social distancing measures and fundamental changes to the nation's spending habits.[2]

As an east Londoner, it was painful to see companies like the baking staple Percy Ingle disappear virtually overnight. Brands such as TM Lewin, Laura Ashley, Cath Kidson, EasyJet, Oliver Sweeney, Debenhams, Oasis, Flybe and Victoria Secret (UK annexe), to name but a few, plunged into bankruptcy, administration, multiple store closures or having to lay off staff after just a few short weeks of being mandatorily closed by the government.

Thousands of people's livelihoods were snatched from underneath their feet due to this ravenous and baleful virus. However, transnational companies like Deliveroo and Amazon, went from strength to strength during the pandemic as they were able to quickly provide for customers who were confined to their homes during our several months of isolation.

Coronavirus became a driver of double-edged change and effects—a marriage between multifaceted loss and at times sociological gain. On the one hand, the tumultuous virus claimed many businesses, jobs and countless lives. But on the other hand, specifically for those with more privilege, people were able to spend more time with their families due to working from home and finally look for a change of career due to a siesta away from their toxic workplaces. Others, interestingly, were able to start that business that remained on the back burner due to the extra hours spare, which would usually otherwise be spent on the central line commuting, or fostered new hobbies that serve the soul, becoming expert gardeners, coffee brewers and banana cake makers.

The pandemic allowed many people to slow down and

steer away from the distractions of everyday life. Not only did it enable many to become thankful for their health, but also, it provided the space away from our usual distractions. For many people, the government mandated lockdown, with no unessential trips (unless you were Dominic Cummings), nights out drinking or fancy dinners provided a stillness that gave birth to a whole host of new emotions and feelings.

As a global community, we were consistently in a state of transition, in and out of lockdown, face masks on, and then off, things open then once more closed again. Transition, in its essence, suggests movement, and in the case of Miss Rona, we remained physically still but transitioned in thought and moved socially, and politically (in some instances).

Whilst the COVID-19 virus impacted everyone, the British government's report on race and COVID-19 revealed that the virus disproportionately impacted Black people. The death rates for ethnic minorities compared to white counterparts were higher and the impact of COVID-19 in relation to the Black community was not just seen in mortality rates. It extended to Black-owned businesses, healthcare access for Black communities, Black employment, Black housing, Black education and more. COVID-19 further exacerbated the already existing inequalities that Black communities faced.

In the height of the pandemic, research began to suggest ethnic minority owned businesses, specifically those who catered to their communities were met with additional pressures of the pandemic.[3]

Before the COVID-19 pandemic, Black business owners already had lower rates of mainstream and government backed business support.[4] When the pandemic hit, nearly two-thirds of Black and minority ethnic business owners felt that it was not possible for them to access government backed assistance, leaving many Black businesses on the edge of destruction.[5]

This period was marked with another major societal change, the murders of George Floyd and Breonna Taylor by police, which resulted in the resurgence of the Black Lives Matter movement. The outrage over the murders would reverberate throughout the world, causing mass global protests. Calls began for governments, businesses and institutions to dramatically improve their treatment of Black people. Corporations were held to task, individuals and brands were held accountable for questionable actions and policies.

Day by day, a new corporation would put out a statement standing with Black people and often highlighting what they would be doing to support the Black community. New Black funds started, Black mentoring schemes began, apologies were offered, crowdfunders, people appeared to be, for the first time in a while, standing with Black people. For those of us who are Black, it was never lost on us that it took the brutal murder of George Floyd and Breonna Taylor for individuals, governments and corporations to publicly stand with Black people.

The seemingly measurable impact the BLM movement had on people's sudden desire to support Black businesses was considered huge. There now appeared to be a global outcry for people to 'Buy Black'. This previously internal conversation had made its way into the mainstream, the biggest businesses, the biggest non-Black celebrities and industries were now appearing to call for the support of Black-owned businesses.

The synergy between the COVID-19 pandemic and the resurgence of the BLM movement in 2020, were both unique and unprecedented in terms of how it impacted Black entrepreneurship and businesses.

The effectiveness of the 2020 wave of the BLM movement led companies to feel that if they too were not loud about their support for the Black community, they would in turn lose the spending power of the Black community as well as the community's ever increasing number of allies.

Celebrities like Kylie Jenner were essentially forced into tagging the Black-owned Loudbrand Studios clothing company on Instagram for free, because the calls from the Black community were loud and consistent. Because of this, we have also seen the emergence of Black support networks, investment for Black businesses, Black Pound Day and so many other initiatives to support Black creatives and businesses.

In John Kotter's book, *Leading Change*, he explains that there are eight clear steps to creating change, both socially and in the workplace. Let us look at Kotter's theory in the context of Black Lives Matter during the COVID-19 pandemic:

- **STEP ONE:** create urgency within groups of people or an organisation, which will, in turn, motivate people to step towards action.

- **STEP TWO:** form a strong coalition with multiple agencies, as for change to happen it has to be well-led.

- **STEP THREE:** develop a vision of change and be clear on how the changes proposed will affect the wider majority.

- **STEP FOUR:** communicate the vision to reach the broadest possible audience via multiple mediums of communication whilst being

honest and tapping into the emotional dimen-
sions of people's fears and concerns.

ə **STEP FIVE:** empower people by removing
barriers, giving them agency to execute the
aforementioned visions of change, which will, in
turn, result in change coming into actualisation.

ə **STEP SIX:** generate short-term outcomes
or 'wins', as Lewin puts it, which will increase
the confidence and experience of those seeking
change.

ə **STEP SEVEN:** desist from resistance, Lewin
acknowledges that with the change, there is
always resistance to the positive changes groups
aim to make. Lewin states that one must not let
up on movements because once momentum is
lost, they are often difficult to regain. Essentially,
strike while the iron is hot.

ə Finally, **STEP EIGHT:** groups must make
these calls to change as systemic failures are
often profoundly set in the fabric of society
and companies, which often make them hard
to break. However, new approaches must be
anchored to see the changes that we want in
both the local and global community.

The Black Lives Matter movement moved through all of these
steps within a matter of weeks. At the time I was working with
an organisation that was able to put together and implement

a whole inclusion campaign for its employees in response to the global outcry in a matter of days. Brands came out with statements of support saying that they are going to foster better practices in all levels of the business. People like Alexis Ohanian, the founder and former CEO of Reddit, altruistically stepped down from his position on the company's board to make space for diverse leaders.

Companies like Shopify publicly acknowledged the systemic barriers faced by Black communities which have prevented their full participation in the entrepreneurial journey, leading them to pledge over £100,000,000 of resources to help create 1,000,000 new Black-owned businesses by 2030. In addition, the e-commerce platform launched the Build Black programme, which is a conversation series that brings together leading Black business minds to discuss start-up culture.

Investment opportunities began emerging to support the ventures of Black entrepreneurs. We saw the emergence of Black-owned groups for Black people buying from one another, and the calling from all groups to support Black businesses.

However, even with this boost in support for Black British business, many challenges remained for Black entrepreneurs. The impacts of the BLM movement did not completely cancel out the effects of being in a global pandemic. In London, there are over 10,000 Black-owned businesses employing one or more staff, accounting for 4% of all London businesses. With Black-owned businesses estimated to account for 6% of all the business across the United Kingdom. During the COVID-19 pandemic, there was roughly a 30% decline in Black-owned business from February to April 2020, despite Black women remaining the fastest growing group of entrepreneurs across the globe.

That is not to say, there weren't a notable amount of success stories because there certainly were. Many Black businesses proved their agility and entrepreneurial creativity and held their ground during the pandemic. Some Black businesses even began amidst the COVID-19 pandemic

Black businesses like Day Like This (DLT), an event based business had to really go back to the drawing board due to the pandemic but co-founder Michael Amunsan admitted the pandemic taught him and his team that they needed to exist in the digital space just as much as the physical space. The pandemic, for his company he explained, made them 'closer, smarter and more selective,' they were able to use the time to reflect and build their business to be even better.

Another business, Hutch, was founded by Sait Cham and launched during the pandemic. On the topic of the impacts the pandemic had on his business, Cham explained that 'COVID supercharged our business, as more people were ordering online.'

Businesses like Black Pound Day, founded by UK artist Swiss from So Solid Crew, work to tackle the economic inequalities that Black businesses face. Black Pound Day hopes to become the largest Black directory and marketplace within Europe. Swiss launched Black Pound Day in June 2020 at the height of the pandemic. It was in direct response to the murders of George Floyd and Breonna Taylor. At the time of writing this book, Black Pound Day now has a physical store in London's Westfield shopping centre.

There are companies like Trapfruits London, founded by Peigh and Baff, who started the business during COVID. Trapfruits is a fruit box delivery service offered either as subscription, re-ordering, or a one off order. In a time where we were all locked in our houses, and everyday items were selling out, the co-founders of Trapfruits London, created an avenue to have healthy eating be more accessible, at a time when everyday food access was extremely inaccessible.

Other companies include Ava Estelle, a Black British skin care company founded by Yaw Okyere that also launched during the pandemic.

Model, body positivity activist and sister author of *A Quick Ting On: Bamboo Earrings* Sophia Tassew is another example of how Black entrepreneurs used the lockdown to their advantage. She started her handmade earring brand Khula store from her bedroom in early 2020. Tassew has since moved into her own design studio, with each collection selling out within minutes of launch.

DRIVING CHANGE

Attracting and maintaining diverse talent throughout an organisation is crucial to a company's success, as it has been shown that companies with a diverse workforce tend to rank higher in workplace well-being, employees tend to feel optimistic about progression and they make more money. Organisations with a diverse team are a win-win. So if diversity leads you down the yellow brick road of success, why aren't more companies fostering inclusion?

In 2020, companies were thrown into existential dread after the death of George Floyd rocked the world at its core. The conversations about systemic racism and how it is insidiously and deeply embedded, some may even say woven intentionally into society, came to a head. Companies were in the spotlight and had to confront the lack of diversity of their employees and more importantly their senior leadership teams.

Between June and November 2020, more posts looking for experts in diversity and inclusion were posted online than in the whole history of the internet. Faux or not, companies suddenly woke up. There were Black inclusion campaigns, Black employee reports, conversations about blind CVs and the list goes on. Companies suddenly wanted more Black staff.

Ultimately, to truly aid Black entrepreneurs, we must support Black businesses. As we mentioned in Chapter 6, the increase in support for Black-owned businesses coming from the murder of George Floyd comes with its own problems. Black trauma is not a viable route for Black people to gain support, there needs to be a less reactive, more sustainable way for consumers to support the Black Business world.

The COVID-19 pandemic, in unison with the response to the Black Lives Matter movement, was a testing time for Black entrepreneurs. It demanded emotional strength, agility and a new kind of resilience. If we were operating in the pandemic without the global outcry of the Black Lives movement, it is very likely that some of the supposed benefits that Black entrepreneurs were able to access wouldn't have existed. Equally, would the outrage of the killings of George Floyd and Breonna Taylor have been felt to the degree they were by the wider non-Black community had we all been outside living lives as usual? Seems unlikely.

What we do know is the almost simultaneous occurrence of these too huge societal moments did impact Black-owned companies and it did so in a variety of ways. Despite there being some clear positive outcomes for the Black community during this time, namely in terms of awareness of racial injustice, a boost of support for Black-Owned businesses, investment, employee work initiatives and social mobility for some Black folk, it remained a double edged sword. Many Black businesses still struggled to stay afloat during this time and COVID-19 impacted the actual livelihood of Black people in a far harsher way than it did others.

Tragically, as previously mentioned, the murder of two Black people—George Floyd and Breonna Taylor was part of the impetus to 'buy Black'. We couldn't catch a break in 2020. The reason for Black people's outcome disparity when it came to COVID mortality rates remains widely debated. Though it is generally accepted that it is a complex mix of societal and structural issues ranging from upstream social and economic inequalities, downstream biological factors, and of course good old medical racism amongst many other things.

So whilst I started this chapter in the height of the pandemic and the resurgence of the BLM movement. I finish the chapter at the start of what everyone is calling the 'cost of living crisis' in the UK. Recent inflation rates for the 12 months to July 2022 reveal that services and goods cost over 10.1% than they did the previous year. Energy regulators have come out claiming there will be up to 80% price hikes of energy bills. The UK is about to enter even more economic turmoil.

Statistics already reveal the cost of living crisis will disproportionately impact Black people, a survey conducted by Censuswide highlighted the racial disparity the cost of living crisis will have on people within the UK.[6] The survey revealed that over a third of those from ethnic minority backgrounds stated they are no longer able to pay their monthly bills, rent or mortgage each month.[7] This in turn resulted in over a quarter of professionals from minority backgrounds considering moving back in with their parents.[8]

The survey also revealed that employees from ethnic backgrounds are almost twice as likely to have been told they won't be receiving a pay rise. This has led to 35% of ethnic minority employees getting into more debt due to taking out loans to deal with the economic crisis.[9]

When it comes to businesses, it has already been reported that businesses are losing confidence in banks[10] and a separate PayPal study revealed that the majority of small business owners in the UK are worried about their business futures.[11]

What we have learned over the course of this book is that when something impacts businesses in general, it tends to impact Black-owned businesses even more.

Only time will tell how the soaring inflation rates and the cost of living crisis will truly impact Black businesses, but we know that it will have a major impact—we will be watching!

9

BUILDING A TOOLKIT

Every entrepreneur needs to have a tool kit. This toolkit should consist of research and a clear strategy on what they want to achieve, but also, help them monopolise on time and increase their productivity. Essentially, when building a personal toolkit you have to spend time to save time.

Personal, is the most important word. The toolkit you curate during your business journey should be unique to you and your business. I know, because I have been there. Ultimately, your toolkit should enable a vision, with that vision constantly being propped up by the toolkit you put together for yourself and employees if you have them.

The reality is, at the start of your entrepreneurship journey and for a long time after—you will be figuring it out as you go along. Learning, experimenting and making mistakes are all part of the baptism of being an entrepreneur.

COMMUNITY:
DLT AND BLACK JOY

At the core of any business is a community. It is the thread that holds it all together, it dictates business decisions and it reminds any business of their why. Businesses cater to communities, they can create communities and have the ability to enhance communities.

One business that very clearly captures the meaning of community is Days Like This, better known as DLT. DLT was founded by Michael Amusan, Bosun Apata and Anthony Iban. Amusan explains that the idea came to the boys when they were on finance internships in New York in 2015. Here they would stumble upon the thriving Black day party scene. 'These spaces made it feel like you were part of a community,' Amusan reflects. The three friends would regularly attend the myriad or Black brunches and day parties throughout the city. They would arrive back in the UK, one year later in 2016. Unlike New York, they realised a rich Black brunch scene did not exist in London. So, they set about to create it.

'AT THE START IT WAS JUST A PARTY FOR OUR FRIENDS'

The boys found a venue in Old Kent Road, and Amusan admits 'it took some convincing' to get the venue owner on board. The idea was relatively new to the London scene, proving the viability of brunch that turns into a party was not a tested concept in the capital of the UK, so venues were sceptical at the start. Nevertheless, the first event in Old Kent Road, managed to draw 300 attendees. For the first official DLT brunch, the boys relied heavily on their social networks— friends mainly. Reflecting back, Amusan stated, 'People loved the concept,' the three boys would do another one in Canary Wharf and the rest is history!

The early days of DLT were very much a DIY endeavour by the founders. They had a twitter and instagram page, for example, but Amusan laughingly admitted they didn't know what they were doing. Fast forward to today, they have a digital team and strong online presence that communicates the needs of their audience.

When asked about the journey of developing the business and concept idea, Amusan says he and his co-founders had the New York Black brunch scene as something to compare their events with, but when it came to the nitty gritty of doing things like booking DJ's, marketing the events, booking venues—they had no clue.

Whilst their financial background didn't grant them knowledge about the art of event curation, it did mean that they were financially savvy. Cleverly managing how they took risks. Interestingly, the co-founders always self-funded their own events and since its inception they have never really made a loss.

Today DLT is a prime space for young Black people to party. Their events sell out almost instantly and it is difficult to find a young Black person living in London who has not attended at least one DLT event.

After some years in, the DLT boys would bring in new talent with specialities across PR, culture, music programming, digital marketing and more. Like many of the businesses in this book, the founders went back to their community to find talent. Amusan highlighted that every person that works within DLT was a prior DLT attendee.

With this expansion of the business, they built on their organic growth, assessing things like programming, DJ line-up and, of course, taking it global. Chris Kutoya, DLT's Team coordinator, speaks to parts of this expansive process when referencing the art of music programming, which is crucial to DLT events. People may assume that it is easy but a lot goes into the music that attendees enjoy at their events.

'YOU CAN THINK "RAH I'M AT A PARTY THE MUSIC IS FLOWING GREAT" BUT YOU DON'T UNDERSTAND HOW MANY MEETINGS GO INTO THAT' —CHRIS KUTOYA

Like Amunsan, Kutoya stressed the importance of involving the next generation. He mentions his younger siblings, who tell him who they listen to, taking their musical recommendations seriously. Importantly he speaks about giving inexperienced DJ's a chance to develop and hone their skills at DLT events. This is a large part of the DLT ethos, bringing in people from the community and giving them a shot. Chris speaks to the value of giving young, often Black, DJ's the chance to have access to the DLT demographic and how positive that is for one's career.

'ONE DAY SOMEONE CAME UP TO US AT ONE OF PARTIES IN LONDON AND SAID YOU SHOULD TAKE THIS TO NIGERIA'

The request to take it outside of the UK, seemed like a challenging thing to execute but their business partner Anthony agreed it would be a good idea. The DLT boys would go on to hold parties in both Nigeria and Ghana in 2019.

DLT for Chris is about 'creating an inclusive safe space for Black professionals' he expands, 'we work so hard in the week, we need to be in spaces with like minded people to have fun.' The DLT family extends to the DJ's, the attendees, the DLT staff, the venues, the sponsors and so much more. They have developed an international network that started from just wanting to provide a lit party for their friends.

So what is the future for DLT? Amusan states, 'we always want to serve our community… It has never been about us, but now more than ever, it is about the people.' He proudly states that the DLT team are all 'anti-keepers'. He and Chris agree that the goal is to have a thriving Black day party scene in the UK whilst, '[breaking] barriers for people after us,' Amunsan says.

PUT YOUR BOOTS ON

You need to be continuously evaluating your toolkit and be open to making changes. Your toolkit will change depending on where you and your business are. Often when starting a business you have no idea of where to start, or you do not have the privilege of being able to save in order to bootstrap your business.

Bootstrap is a term used to describe when an entrepreneur runs out into the abyss of entrepreneurship with nothing but a plan, a cup of ambition, a sprinkle of well wishes and, if they are lucky, their own private savings to fund the business. The first business I started at university was an online magazine for students to get experience in journalism, which quickly turned into a triad of magazines focussing on pop culture, mental health and the politics of growing up. When I started that business I was working part-time at Victoria's Secret Bond Street and I used £200 of my paycheck to get going. Because it was an online blog, it was pretty inexpensive. I bought a domain and set up a Wordpress account under it. From there I bought a theme online and the business was born.

Unsurprisingly, Black founders bootstrap their companies at a higher rate than white or Asian founders — not by choice, but because they often can not get access to venture funding with ease. Three quarters of the founders I have spoken to for this book bootstrapped their businesses, managed to secure grants or used platforms such as Kickstarter to introduce the public to their offering.

YOU CAN NEVER DO TOO MUCH

You can never know too much when it comes to running a business. Because of that, research is key. You must try and find out everything there is to know about your market and targeted demographic.

Many entrepreneurs become entrepreneurs because they have come across a problem and are endeavouring to create or contribute to solving it. Take me, for example, I created my footwear brand because as a taller girl with larger feet I struggled to find footwear that was my size and looked good. So, I created a footwear company that catered to that need, thereby filling a gap in the market.

I am learning new things every single day about shoe design and manufacturing, but the early days of the brand's inception was a hustle. I had no idea about fashion design, so I started by buying an infinite amount of shoes, tearing them apart and inspecting them. I wanted to build a sustainable brand so I stayed up late studying materials and what certain materials meant for the environment. I knew I would be creating a truly inclusive brand that would cater to all, free from gendered marketing, which meant I had to learn about the history of fashion and why it came to be gendered in the way that it is.

I leaned on the LGBTQ+ community and paid various consultants that were part of that community to make sure that my messaging would resonate in the right way with all consumers. I had to try, fail, go back and research ways to ensure that the heels on my shoes could carry people of all weights comfortably and safely—the first few heels fell off—we cannot have that happening when someone is giving it their all on the Ballroom floor!

In true novice style, I didn't take into consideration that industries change, trends change, markets change, audiences change—so you, as an entrepreneur need to make sure that even once you are established that your research never stops because there are always new developments in business that require understanding.

I am continuously researching ways to make the brand even more sustainable. I am constantly buying and testing different materials made from various recycled plants and plastics. I go to visit the factories where my shoes are made to ensure that the factory and its managers are treating their workers correctly and are not negatively impacting the local environment or worse. Whether your research is done at your desk, or you are going out and learning more from a position of lived experience it is important to remember that we are forever scholars when it comes to entrepreneurship.

SOCIAL MEDIA

Social media is great. It has changed the way we receive and disseminate information. Each platform has its functions and uses, Twitter seems to have become a news source, which is both a good and bad thing. Instagram has become a shopping outlet, which has done nothing but affect my savings. Using social media is important for any business, as it allows you to connect with your audience and gives you the opportunity to play with the authentic voice that every brand should have. But, social media trends are always changing and ten years ago we would have never guessed that Instagram would have become a marketplace and Twitter, oftentimes, a rawer and more trustworthy news source than the TV channels.

So, with that in mind it is important to get as much information about your customers as possible, so they can stay connected with you no matter how much social media pivots. One way that I encourage people to do this is by building a mailing list. An email list, put simply, is just a list of email addresses gathered from visitors that opt in to receiving information, updates and discounts from your brand or service. Having an email list is important as email marketing is the best way to stay connected with your customers outside of traditional social media.

According to management and marketing consultancy firm McKinsey and Company, email marketing is six times more successful at acquiring new customers for a brand than Facebook or Twitter and they found that your brand is six times more likely to get higher click-through rates through using email rather than tweets. You might think that mailing lists are archaic or for the 419 scammers but it is actually a wonderful way to stay in touch with your customers. Mailing lists stand the test of time. I cannot see the foreseeable death of emails, but I can see the death of an app like Instagram. By building a mailing list, no matter what area of business you are in, you can remain in touch with the audience that you have spent years building.

AGILITY AND CURIOSITY

The ability to maintain a culture and strategy that continues to add value, especially when operating in uncertain and murky environments is key. As is the constant desire to know more and learn more. The world of business is far from stagnant, it is ever changing and so as entrepreneurs it means we also have to be. Being curious helps hugely.

Sait Cham is founder of Hutch. Hutch builds services and products to help small to medium e-commerce brands delight their customers—they specifically focus on the post-purchase experience. Their customers use Hutch's fulfilment services to ship products to customers and use their suite of products to retain customers.

On why he is an entrepreneur, Cham states, 'It's the one job that allows me to obsessively explore all my curiosities. I really enjoy problem solving, I enjoy being creative, I enjoy building a team and culture of people I really like, I like learning a lot, I like freedom, I like control over my destiny and I want to make a lot of money.' An agile and curious entrepreneur if there ever was one.

Cham launched his business in the midst of the pandemic, a challenging and unique time that presented his business and many businesses with a very difficult set of circumstances. Nevertheless, his business adapted to the times. When asked about his company's ethos he explained, 'We're on a mission to become the best post-purchase solution for customer-centric e-commerce brands worldwide. We strongly believe e-commerce will become the primary method of buying goods and services in the future. Our vision is to be at the forefront of that change and ensure we're playing our part in ensuring consumers receive the greatest experience possible!'

Adapting to external changes during the pandemic, such as a working from home culture, new health and safety guidelines, constant government changes and being a new business during this time is what an agile business is all about. It allows the business and leadership to evolve with the times.

NETWORKS AND MOBILITY

A 'network' makes a great addition to your toolkit. In 1997, Sociologist Anthony Heath and Doreen McMahon coined the term 'ethnic penalty', which was conceived as the lower chances, lack of opportunities and higher risks of unemployment for an equally qualified member of a minority ethnic group, when compared with the white majority. Later, in the extensive report 'Class matters: a study of minority and majority social mobility in Britain' (2016), written by Heath and research colleague Yaojun Li, the connection between the way in which social mobility and economic opportunities interact framed our understanding of racial inequality, with class and race being the two protected factors that are passed on generationally. Highlighting that a new radical approach needs to be taken to the ways in which those of Caribbean and African descent are able to strengthen both their class and social mobility in Britain.

Li and Heath found that Black British women and men are particularly likely to experience downwards mobility. Full-time employment rates for Black women fell 15-20% over a decade whilst the employment position of white women remained stable; not to mention the unemployment rates for Black men remained triple that of their white counterparts for the past 20 years. They also found that racial discrimination affected the first and second generations alike. Despite often having a better education than their white counterparts, both generations of Black Britons failed to secure occupational positions that corresponded with their human capital, which is even more alarming for the second generation who were indeed educated here in Britain.[1]

When I think about the term 'ethnic penalty', I am drawn

to the specific factors that could hinder social mobility, and especially how a parent or guardian can secure employment gateways or internships for their children. In 2009, every major political party in Britain was focused on this point. Liberal Democrat Leader Nick Clegg was first out the gate and set up a commission to look at social mobility in the UK. The commission was chaired by Barnardo's Chief Executive Martin Narey at the time and found that 'a child's prospects are tied to the circumstances of their birth.'[2] Ten years later, in 2019, the longitudinal findings remain consistent that, 'being born privileged still means you usually remain privileged.'[3] Even though it is a matter of statistical fact and remains unsurprising for those who are born out of privilege, social mobility remains a talking point in political debate, lecture theatres and dinner tables across Britain.

The Social Mobility Commission's report, chaired by Dame Martina Milburn and entitled 'State of Nation Social Mobility in Britain', highlights that 'social mobility has remained virtually stagnant since 2014,' and 'even when those from working-class backgrounds are successful in entering professional occupations, they earn on average 17% less than their more privileged colleagues.'[4] In regard to enterprise, the findings are the same. Even though the level of entrepreneurial activity is growing in the Black community, its owners often struggle to get the investment needed to grow their businesses. Research conducted by Transparent Collective found that less than 1% of all Venture Capital funding is granted to Black-owned businesses, with disparities even wider for those born of lower socioeconomic status.[5] So what can be done?

Short answer. Multi-faceted networks that cover funding, professional development and relationships. For example, in 2019, Impact X, a Black-owned and managed venture capital fund launched to invest £100,000,000 into Black-owned businesses across the United Kingdom and Europe. Impact X hopes to help grow and support under-represented groups with the funds and connections needed to start a successful business. Impact X, amongst a growing number of venture capital funds, are putting together toolkits to help Black entre-preneurs thrive.

Kike Oniwinde, the founder of Black Young Professionals Network (BYP), is changing 'the Black narrative' by bringing the Black professional community together to solve our own problems through mentoring, job opportunities, economic empowerment and connectivity. BYP believes that 'your network is your net worth' and helps Black Young Professionals navigate the corporate world whilst showing up as their authentic selves.

With thousands of members across the globe, they provide their audience with a tailored social network, professional development blogs, leadership podcasts and events to bolster their career. I am particularly inspired by BYP Network, as the core of the business seems to harness the communal power of our oral traditions and histories, holding community at the centre but bringing it to the new world—the internet age.

In 5 short years, BYP has amassed over 40,000 active members and 60 corporate partners including Facebook and Accenture. For too long, corporations have relied on its employees' personal connections in order to fill open vacan-cies, this technique overwhelmingly excludes Black people from the hiring process.

Other companies like Social FIXT are also using social media platforms as a means to build networks for Black people. Founded by Mercedes Benson, esteemed DJ and social entrepreneur, Social FIXT is a disruptive recruitment and job-board that aims to connect Black talent to jobs within the creative industry. The platform was born out of Benson's own experiences, as it was a rarity for Benson to work on projects with people who looked like her, spoke like her, shared her interests, and had similar experiences.

The lack of diversity and frames of reference coupled with conversations she would have with friends who worked in the industry too led to the birth of Social FIXT. All of the jobs, apprenticeships and internships posted on the website are hand selected by Benson and her team, and vetted first to ensure that the companies are places that value diversity and inclusion, have robust employee development programmes and, of course, pay well!

Anthropologist Ilana Gershon, in her paper 'Down and out in the new economy: how people find (or don't find) work today', argues that 'some [professional] jobs depend entirely on being able to turn your friends and acquaintances into business opportunities' for oneself, stating 'nowadays almost all the time the job applications are online,' meaning that a recruiter is more likely to look at a candidates LinkedIn profile instead of a traditional CV, and 'social media presence as a basis for screening their job application.'[6] Even though this seems to be a simpler and technologically contemporary way to hire folk, it actually limits Black applicants' access, especially when the majority of staff already tend to be white, meaning that their networks, typically, tend to be other white people. This is why networks like BYP are so important, they enable Black entrepreneurs to use their social mobility to support one another.

Companies like Hustle Crew, founded by Abadesi Osunsade are also helping bridge the gap and make workplaces more inclusive. Hustle Crew has a network of over 5,000 under-represented professionals, but also run B2B workshops to teach high-impact tools and frameworks so companies can optimise for inclusion in every decision, from hiring to design. The company believes that learning is a process of building blocks, and 'thinking is a habit, and like any other habit, it can be changed; it just takes effort and repetition.'

This quote by John Elliot was plucked from the Hustle Crew website and sums up why continual learning is so important for businesses. For example, their workshops teach employees about bias, privilege and structural oppression. Whilst, helping them to explore how to be proficient in optimising for diversity. Essentially, Hustle Crew provides companies with their own personalised toolkit and methodology to build an inclusive company culture which by osmosis and extension helps build inclusive networks for employees.

During a conversation with Osunsade, she spoke about the importance of networking and how 'sharing or inviting people into our network can be one of the biggest gifts we can give each other' as Black entrepreneurs and leaders. I started to think about 'the old boys' network' and the ways in which they have been able to maintain that network due to the way in which they converse and build relationships with one another. Those relationships are built over intimate dinners, behind the closed doors of private members clubs. Deals are made over glasses of Tignanello and Japanese whiskey. They have their own closed community, where they share resources, contacts, job offers and even capital with one another. We must do the same.

NO MAN IS AN ISLAND

Self-reflection is critical. Sadly, having the feeling that you would make a good leader, or just wanting to work for your-self because you hate taking instructions, or coming up with a start-up idea at 10pm whilst intoxicated is not going to cut it. Everything in your toolkit needs to be researchable and measurable.

Now, I am not saying that in order to start a business you need to have been in a formal managerial position, but there should be noted moments where you can say you have been pensive, reflective and an active listener whilst under pressure. Please note, this is more than just listening to your parents nagging you and resisting the urge to tell them to shut up. I am also not saying that you cannot develop these skills, you definitely can, but you have to be an actively self-aware person with an open willingness to be emotionally flexible and honest with yourself. Because if you cannot be honest with yourself then this entrepreneur thing may not be for you. It took me a long time to be honest with myself, especially when it came to my own business.

'I CAN'T COME AND KILL MYSELF...'
—A NIGERIAN SAYING*

I wanted to do everything for myself: the designing, the distribution, the social media, the shipping, all whilst working full-time as a consultant to sustain myself. I beg, do not let being a control freak ruin you. It took me two years to realise that I could not do it all myself so I saved up so that I could hire a small team to help me. One frontier was social media. I know the strategy and how to monetize it, but actually having to post was just a chore that would continually push me to the edge. So I got myself a Social Media Director and hired my 13 year old niece to help with shipping and emails.

A problem I had been struggling with for two plus years was fixed randomly one evening, when I looked in the mirror and was willing to accept that I truly was not an island, and in order to get my business off the ground I had to relinquish

---

* Not meant to be interpreted in a literal sense but reflects one's attitude when frustrated, overworked, tired or is said when one accepts defeat.

some control. Because of this self-reflection, the business is doing better and guess what, I am less stressed! So make sure that you are continuously checking in with yourself. It should not take you as long as it took me to be honest with yourself. Money is time and time is money, baybie.

SELF-CARE AS A RADICAL TOOL

The foundation of your toolkit should be self-care. You should not forget about or neglect your personal toolkit, which should include all the things that ensure your personal wellbeing. Being an entrepreneur, especially a Black one, can be extremely difficult. There are also other factors that add to the challenge: if you are diversely-abled, LGBTQ+, are a parent or carer, have alternative learning needs, you identify as a woman and a myriad of other diversities. That is why it is paramount to centre and ground yourself. One entrepreneur I spoke to, who has asked to remain anonymous, had this to share:

> 'I worked for an investment bank and then started my business, but that did not prepare me for the stresses. I was working all night, I didn't take a break from the business for months. I missed loved ones' birthdays and weddings, my romantic and familiar relationships started to break down and slowly I started to use alcohol as a coping mechanism. I decided to get support and outsource after I gave a speech whilst drunk. I share this not to scare you, but to show where it can go if you refuse to centre yourself like I did. You know the old saying right: you can't pour from an empty cup...'

I was so thankful that I was trusted with this experience and was given permission to document this moment of candour for this chapter. Statistically non-white people often do not have the economic leverage or resources to outsource expertise or hire staff early on in their business journey. This leads to all types of stresses, and it can seem like each day, hour and minute collapses into each other with no moment to breathe. I know at times, even until today, I feel like I am in a rat-race where ironically I am the only contestant and the only one who knows where the finish line is.

This is my signal to pause and re-evaluate. I only feel like this once in a blue moon, and it usually arises when I have not been feeding my soul, which often consists of: a day/s away from my desk, socialising with friends, kickboxing, seeing my family, some extravagant skincare purchases, reading, therapy and working on my knee strength so one day I can twerk in a low squat like Meg Thee Stallion. That is my self-care.

'Self-care' is defined as things we deliberately partake in, which in turn consecrates our physical, emotional and mental health. Coined in the 1950s, this medical term was used by practitioners to describe activities that helped mental health patients preserve some physical independence, as it was found that small simple acts like going for a walk and personal grooming made patients more productive and improved their sense of self-worth. However, it was not until the civil rights movement that the term self-care became a political act of service for oneself and the wider community. By taking stock of their health and wellbeing, Black people, more specifically Black women, were able to protest against white supremacist medical systems that often excluded them.

Audre Lorde, Black feminist, poet and civil rights activist, in her book of essays entitled *Burst of Light* stated that:

'Caring for [one]self is not self-indulgence, it is
self-preservation, and that is an act of political
warfare.'[7]

More recently, Natalia Mehlman Petrzela, an assistant pro-
fessor at the New School explained that the political appropri-
ation of the term self-care was a way to claim 'autonomy over
the body as a political act against institutional, technocratic,
very racist, and sexist [structures].'[8] When I think about the
business world in particular, there are so many factors that
exclude people on the basis of their gender, race, ability and
more notably class.

I maintain that class is the bottom of the pyramid of inequality as this factor transcends all of the other intersections.
If you grow up in economic deprivation, you are more likely
to have worse health outcomes, if you are not physically and
mentally well you are therefore more likely to miss out on
education, and employment—sure as hell, your chances of
running a fruitful business are also limited.

The radical break in self-care can be attributed to the
transatlantic slave trade, where work and survival came first
and self-care thereafter. A typical plantation slave worked 12
or more hours a day 'from day clean to first dark,'[9] six days
a week and would 'invariably [have] the Sunday off unless
during harvest [season].'[10] During their free time, they would
invest in self-care, which usually centred around their hair.
'Slaves devised hair care tools, such as using wool carding tools
to comb through tangles,' whilst 'men used axle grease as both
a dye and relaxer.'[11] The legacy of work before self-care is
rooted in a complex trans-generation experience. As much as
this is about race, it is also about class.

My mother was obsessed with the boxset *Pride and Prejudice*
when I was growing up, and no matter how many times we

watched it, I was always taken aback by how much time they spent combing their hair or doing gentle needlework. The upper-classes, since the beginning of time, have had practices of self-care, whilst those with little resources tried their best to get by, much like contemporary society. Working-class Black people in the UK are more likely to work two jobs, look after their families or loved ones full-time, or sometimes do both— leaving very little time for self-care. A lot of Black start-up entrepreneurs, do all the above and run a business—it is a lot.

Personally, taking time out for self-care has been a frontier for me as a leader and entrepreneur. But the thing that has helped me be slightly more fastidious with my 'self-care' has been getting my hair professionally done once a month. Chloe Robinson, the founder of Heroine Hair Salon, is one of my 'self-care custodians', and promotes to her customers that 'self care is political and is one way to demonstrate to yourself that you matter,' but it is especially important to her as a Black woman as society is structured in a way to make us question our self worth.

For Robinson, hairdressing is a form of therapy, with clients opening up to her 'in a way that they have expressed they would not open up to their family or friends.' In her words 'there is something intrinsically psychological about talking to someone standing behind them whilst they sit in front of a mirror' as they have to look at themselves and the hair stylist as a reflection—leaving space, well at least for me, the opportunity to confront and reflect on myself. This is why no matter how hard it is Black entrepreneurs should take time to foster a culture to look after themselves—whether it be regular trips to the salon, taking holidays, lying in bed binge-watching a series or simply doing nothing—self-care is one of the most important parts of our toolkit.

By implementing self-care into your routine and trying

to put your best foot forward—where you can—you begin to slowly chip away and dismantle the hierarchies of race, gender, sexuality and class inequality. By doing this you not only look after yourself but your whole community. Look after you first.

10

THE FUTURE OF OUR LEGACY—FROM ALLYSHIP TO 'REVOLUTION'

So here we are friends, you have stayed with me to the very end. The final chapter of any book is an important one, it brings everything together. In this case, we must end a book on Black entrepreneurship centring the important topic of Legacy.

When Jay-Z released his *4:44* album the final song on the album was named 'Legacy', the song starts with the iconic voice of Blue Ivy asking her father, 'Daddy what's a will?' The song reflects on generational Black wealth, his entrepreneurial endeavours and passing it down. The concept of legacy is a romanticised one, specifically in our community, I think in part because so many have tried to destroy the existence of Black legacy. When we think of the word legacy, specifically Black legacy, this book series is a good example, it has created something that will last, something that provides long term opportunity for those involved and those who are inspired by it.

Throughout the book I have spoken to entrepreneurs who have created beautiful Black legacies, through the media space, the beauty space, the tech space, the online space, the activism space and more. As we have seen, community has proved to be at the core of so many Black entrepreneurial endeavours and where there is community, there is always legacy.

So what is Black Legacy and how does one even begin to describe it?

Is it leaving something behind?

Is it building something that inspires, that lasts?

Is it creating generational joy, wealth, access, inspiration and more?

Is it more about creating spaces, building our own tables, planting seeds?

Is it about creating, moving, shaping culture?

The answer is yes to all the above and then some.

As explored in Chapter Two: The History of Black Brit-ish Businesses, the rich legacy of Black British entrepreneurship and resilience is ever present. From Black Tudors like John Blanke and Edward Swarthye to the 18th century entrepreneur Ignatius Sancho all the way to the creative and spirited entrepreneurs of the Windrush generation—the Black British entrepreneurial legacy has been here—inspiring us to this very day. What was achieved by these entrepreneurs was often done against a backdrop of systemic racism and extreme hostility, but the savvy and determined entrepreneurs persevered, carving out new lanes and opportunities.

When we reflect on today's Black entrepreneurial world we must remember that we have come from a long line of entre-preneurs, who set up shop creating pubs, hair shops, salons, barbershops, trading businesses, magazines, radio stations, music labels, book stores, restaurants and so much more.

Before we continue, I have a confession—in the middle of writing this book, I almost gave up on my own business and this research. The challenges seemed too great. Every day I would wake up and there would be a new obstacle, a door I had to kick down or a mountain I had to climb. I was phys-ically, mentally and emotionally exhausted. I wanted to quit my job, grab my passport, max out my American Express card and run off to Mexico. The plan? To change my name, live on a farm, perfect my Spanish and grow perfect organic fruit and vegetables in the sun.

'Til this day, I wonder if I would have actually gone if we were not in the midst of a ravishing global pandemic. All I knew is that I wanted to run. But instead, I sat in the corner of my home office, wept with a chocolate crunchy bar in my hand, bonnet sliding off towards the floor whilst asking myself why I started all of this. Why could I have not just minded my business instead of starting one?

Despite all the accolades and successes I had achieved, I felt like a monumental failure. I questioned whether I was the right person to do this work and whether I actually had it in me to reach the lofty ambitions I had set out for myself. I would let my team down, my publisher down, my family and friends who believed in me down. Throughout my career, I have always challenged people to think about their actions and 'reasons for doing.'

I ask them hard questions like: how do you know you are a good leader? What makes you equipped to run this business? Are you willing to follow through no matter the challenge? But on that day, I would not have been able to adequately answer those questions myself. I did not feel like a good leader, I sure as hell did not feel equipped to run a business and the fact I was crying in a small corner demonstrated very clearly to me that at that time I did not have the tenacity to follow through whatever the circumstance.

As I wiped away my tears with the sleeve of my jumper, I looked up at my bookshelf and my eyes became transfixed. On all fours, I crawled towards the shelf, shuffled onto my knees, stretched out my arm with what felt like the last of my strength and took down a text by Frantz Fanon. Being one of my university texts, it was filled with colourful bookmarking indexes and post-it notes. I flicked through the pages and with sore eyes began to read my previously highlighted and annotated musings. In an almost prophetic note to self, was my handwriting on a yellow post-it note in purple biro:

> 'It is f****** deep. Morrison said the function of racism is distraction and Fanon said that the oppressed will always think the worst about themselves. Black self-doubt is driven by the white supremist [*sic*] capitalist system... kill doubt... leave capitalism.'

I had empirical evidence that I was good at my job, I was a thoughtful leader and had it in me to build a successful business, but the fact that the world was designed to profit and benefit whiteness, maleness and those with the most wealth was weighing me down. It was imposter syndrome—not my incompetence. I was more than competent. I had a job to do. I had a *legacy* to build. I had something to contribute to the world. I had a duty to my Blackness, my womanhood and working-class background. I remembered that I do this not only for myself, but in the hopes that one little Black child might stumble across what I have done and be inspired.

I dried my eyes and remembered that as Black entrepreneurs we are not only mirrors for the next generation, we are builders and carpenters. We are moulding concrete steps for other Black people to climb high, free of burden and unreasonable obstacles. We are etching unshakeable tables, so that other Black people may take a rightful seat. We are just small parts of a long and larger rich history. So, I ask all Black entrepreneurs and leaders, longstanding, new or those with just an idea: What will be your offering to our legacy?

As a community we spend 4% more money annually than any other race, despite being the least represented race and one of the most poverty-stricken in the UK. During one of my favourite sporadic FaceTime calls with Andy Davis, he watched as I embarked on my 7-step skincare routine. He asked me questions about the brands, how much they cost, how many other products I had tried before settling on the ones I was applying. He asked if I had recommended them to a friend and how often I buy them. At first, I thought he was just interested in the elaborate nature of my daily routine. But as the questions progressed I could see that Andy was itching to ask me something else and it was his final question that forever shifted my thinking.

He leaned into the camera, hands clasped solid into an assured fist and asked: how many of those products that you lather on your face are Black-owned? I lowered my head in shame, and in a hushed tone answered, 'None.' Andy did not have to say anything after that, he could tell I had received his subtle communiqué. He made me question why I did not seek out the Black-owned version of Sunday Riley or La Mer. As someone who consistently harps on about reinvesting our hard earned money back into the community, I was not actively ensuring that something Black-owned was in every room, cupboard and most importantly in the skincare fridge in my house. Andy held me accountable and made me question every skincare purchase I have ever made.

There are other marginalised communities that look to their own first. They line the pockets of their own by any means necessary. So, I had to ask myself the hard question of why I was not doing the same? Today, my skincare fridge, hair care routine and sanitary products consist of Black-owned brands like Afrocenchix, Kaike, Monshea, Base+, Bevel, EPARA, Honey Pot and more.

If you have gotten this far into the book you have learnt how many Black businesses and households have been denied the path to wealth accumulation, which is why it is of utmost importance that Black people and allies reinvest their money when they can into Black-owned businesses. Now I get it, it is easy to get caught up in the bustle of everyday life and buy what is the most visible but let us be more conscious with where we put our coins.

Instead of heading to Ikea for a desk, head to a multiplex e-commerce platform like Etsy and check out a Black-owned store. Go for brunch with the homies at that new authentic Bajan restaurant in Croydon. Commission a Black artist for family portraits.

Open a tab and search for 'Black-owned grocery stores in my area'. Pledge part of your salary to platforms like Kwanda, designed to both help and encourage individuals to give back and build within the Black community. Sign up for a Jamii card, which provides discounts for hundreds of Black-owned businesses. Be sure to partake in Black Pound Day. Share this book, buy other books from Black-owned bookstores. Support Black-owned magazines, radio stations, clothing lines, bars. Stop right now and do something ultra-practical for the Black community. These small steps can go a long way. So let's get on with it!

Ozwald Boateng OBE, who I look up to as a reflective and thoughtful uncle of sorts, has consistently remained grounded in his Ghanaian roots. Besides being one of my fashion idols he is a renowned pioneer best known for his trademark twist on classic bespoke tailoring. He was the first tailor to have a catwalk show at Paris Fashion Week in 1994 and used a video promotion as the invitation—visionary, am I right? From this moment on, Boateng did not look back.

At the young age of 28, he opened a retail store on the illustrious Savile Row making him the youngest tailor to adorn the street. In 2003, Boateng became the first Black creative director of the fashion couture house Givenchy. He has been the first of many things and he attributes it to his continuous remembrance and homage to his native homeland Ghana. Boateng has been able to spark a balance between his heritage and quintessential Britishness, through unremittingly refusing to forget his home.

In our conversation for this book, he suggested to me that his power, creativity and thoughtfulness lies in his genealogy and I have to agree. In order to forge a legacy, it is important to acknowledge those that came before us and those that stand as contemporaries. Boateng keeps a watchful eye on West African creativity and cites the innovation in the area not only as inspiration but as a space for us to observe what creative excellence looks like. Through his work and grass-roots activism he aims to unite Africans in a common vision of transforming the continent's roads, railways, power supply and creative industries.

He wants Africa to understand what it can do for itself, after so many centuries of being pillaged and abused for its natural resources.[1] For Black people to realise their potential and power. Boateng gracefully shared that the moment he became a father he truly understood all of the parables and teachings his father bestowed upon him as a young man. In his own words, he truly became a man for the first time, because he could now see the importance of investing in his daughter's cultural self-confidence as a legacy not only for his personal pride but for the wider community.

So, for us to create a legacy we must also be willing to support our legacy, feed our legacy, *buy* from our legacy. If the Black community collectively employs their purchasing power towards Black-owned businesses—we are providing an avenue for the creation of Black prosperity. Now, Black prosperity, whilst it does include financial freedom, does not exclusively mean that. It includes Black health, charity, employment, well being and education. It gives us a chance at recreating our world, from one that is so deeply embedded in racism to something possibly different.

When we harken back to the Windrush generation who came to Britain and completely redesigned Black British entrepreneurship, we saw that their business success didn't end with them. No, it continued throughout their communities. People like Oswald 'Columbus' Denniston, Val McCalla, Len Dyke, Dudley Dryden and Tony Wade created businesses that had huge communal value for the wider Black community, not only that but they also gave back to the community they were part of. This is Black prosperity. Creating success, wealth and opportunities for yourself and your community.

SELF BELIEF—A CAMERA AND A DREAM

When me and the creator of the series, Mags, discussed who should be interviewed for this book, there was one person whose name came up straight away. This person was an instant choice. Why? Because he inhabits the essence of what this book is about: Black creativity, community, resilience, hard work and love. When we speak about Black legacy, he is *it*. He is my late dear friend Jamal Edwards MBE.

Edwards is a great example of what it means to do the inner work first and lead with heart. After being gifted a video camera for Christmas from his mum, he started the culturally disruptive SBTV to connect with other young Black men who shared his common interest in grime music and video making. Edwards wanted other people to feel empowered by their penmanship, and through this SBTV became a platform for ingenious homegrown Black British music talent.

SBTV was an early adopter of a generation that consumed music content online by harnessing the power of YouTube before the industry realised it was a haven for fresh, new talent and creativity. SBTV emboldened underground talent to just put themselves out there without a label or representation, putting on the likes of Ed Sheeran, Jessie J, Stormzy, Dave and Rita Ora to name but a few (and there are many!).

It has been almost 15 years since the launch of SBTV, but Edwards did not stop seeking out opportunities to empower the next generation through working with schools and charities. Edwards was one of the humblest people I had the privilege to know, and one of my main cheerleaders during the journey of writing this book. He was a powerhouse, but was always taken aback when people asked for his opinion and input. It is this humility that enabled him to transform lives and an industry that was, and often remains, gatekept by white executives exploiting Black talent. His legacy is doing the work without thinking of oneself first and most importantly providing a soapbox for a community that is often misunderstood and forgotten by the mainstream.

On the day of his vigil, there were more than 100 people in attendance, and I was overwhelmed by how so many people were able to come together, mourn and share a story about his grace. There were friends and family, but also people who he had offered work to when no one else would, young people he had supported with internships and counsel, alongside people who admired his work from a far.

I have come to terms that my grieving for Jamal may never leave me, but if there is one thing that brings me back from that sorrow is remembering the amount of love and care he poured into the world and our lives. He created a legacy many could only dream of, and there should be celebration and joy in that.

> ### 'LEGACY FOR ME MEANS SETTING UP GREAT FOUNDATIONS FOR OTHERS TO BE INSPIRED.'
> ### —JAMAL EDWARDS.

In our conversation Edwards told me that when it came to business legacy, he didn't have anything to look at or be inspired by growing up. Something that many of us can relate to, but he found solace in the fact that today's generation could now see people like him and realise that they could do it too. To Edwards legacy meant everything, in fact most of our conversation was centred around his hopes and dreams to inspire the next generation. This is the kind of person Edwards was, he put community first. In his own words, 'inspiring the next generation of entrepreneurs is something that is so important to me.'

He spoke about his impetus to create SBTV, which he said came from his frustration 'with mainstream media platforms not featuring the talent that I wanted.' It was about 'problem solving.' Importantly, he says the root of it was also his 'mates' who were struggling to find places to showcase their music. Edwards highlighted that for upcoming musicians at the time 'there wasn't a clear route of how to get on'—so what did he do? He created one. The motivation of Jamal's entrepreneurial journey, like so many Black entrepreneurs, was *community*.

'I KEEP MY HEAD DOWN AND TRY AND WORK AS MUCH AS POSSIBLE.' —JAMAL EDWARDS

What comes across in our chat is Edwards' dedication to helping young people and interestingly not just in his area of expertise. Edwards admitted his area is music but expressed that when young people would enquire about how to get involved in things outside of music, he would use his social mobility to create space and connect young people to enter the careers of their choice.

'What's my legacy in the next 5-10 years?' Edwards asked himself in our conversation, he paused before telling me that he is still looking to learn more and strive for even better. To my surprise, despite all he had achieved he still felt he had a long way to go. I asked him where he sees the next 15 years going, and he told me it's about 'going back.' He spoke about three places that are close to his heart—Acton (where he was raised), Luton (where he was born) and St Vincent (where his family are from).

He spoke passionately about giving back to these communities, wanting to create spaces for young people to reach their potential. In Acton, for example, Edwards started his youth project called Jamal Edwards Delve (JED), where he would work with Google and the Wellcome trust to repurpose old community centres into vibrant youth centres, something that he had hoped to take to boroughs across London and also back home in St Vincent.

Edwards was very much at the apex of successful entrepreneurship, he was a founder of a multi-million pound company, who was charismatic, adored, and a man behind a lot of people's careers. A young entrepreneur who created something unimaginable that inspired a generation. He was awarded an MBE from the Queen, he was listed one of *TIME* magazine's Next Generation Leaders, he was awarded an honorary MBA from Luton & Bedfordshire University, he was a British Interactive Media Association (BIMA) Hall of Famer and the accolades do not stop there. Yet Jamal Edwards felt like he was just getting started and at the time of our interview he expressed that in the next few years he would focus on developing his own content and building himself as a director.

Amazingly, our conversation was not about his achievements (of which he has plenty), his accolades (of which he has plenty) and the people he put on (of which there were many). It was about his hopes for the future, specifically how he could help the next generation. This is the kind of guy Jamal Edwards was—selfless, community-led and giving.

Jamal Edwards, achieved all of this by the age of 31. Alongside his community work and outreach, he was also an author, writing his own book *Self Belief: The Vision: How to Be a Success on Your Own Terms*. The book itself is an extension of his ethos—a six level guide that helps the reader get to the entrepreneurial place they desire to be.

To honour Jamal Edwards, his mother launched The Jamal Edwards Self Belief Trust. The Trust focuses on three areas that were important to Jamal Edwards 1) Tackling homelessness 2) Supporting people with mental health issues and 3) Providing young people with essential life skills. The trust continues to build on Edwards' legacy, ensuring that his work continues.

Jamal Edwards was a modern day entrepreneur, who built something massive from curious passion and the will to change things for the better. In the process he touched the lives of so many. The UK music industry owes a lot to Jamal Edwards, so many artists, videographers, producers are able to trace their journeys to Jamal Edwards carving out space for them to express their art. Jamal did all of this for *us*. He rewrote the script, changed the game and did so with a smile on his face. He used the internet brilliantly, and at a time where the industry was turning its back on Black British musicians, Edwards gave them a platform.

Humble, passionate and grateful—in our interview, Jamal Edwards never gloated about the impressive business he built, the huge impact he had or the artists he helped put on—he instead wanted to talk about giving back to his community, his dreams for his community and his hopes for the next generation of entrepreneurs and creatives. A shining example of Black British entrepreneurship, creativity and strength.

REST IN POWER JAMAL EDWARDS—YOU WILL NEVER BE FORGOTTEN.

INTERVIEW TRANSCRIPTION WITH JAMAL EDWARDS

(This interview has been edited for clarity and consicion.)

TSKENYA-SARAH FRAZER: So in this chapter, I really want to document people who have really contributed positively to the landscape of Black British business in the UK. You've [have contributed so much] in such a short amount of time and you're a baby boy still. So I really want to talk to you about what you envision for the next years of your life... Why is it so important to you to leave a legacy?

JAMAL EDWARDS: Legacy is important to me. I always say young people of today are the future leaders of tomorrow... my mum was obviously a very hard worker...

TSF: She's got a voice!

JE: But that wasn't passed on down to me, I can't sing (laughs)... So in terms of business legacy, there wasn't really anything I could look to or be inspired by. So that's why I always look at me now for the young people of today... [and hope] they would look at my story and be inspired by it. I get messages every week from young people. Just a couple of days ago, I got a message from... a secondary school in Luton (Lee Manor High School) that wants to name one of their buildings after me and I'm just like bloody hell you're going on like I've passed [away]... They have recently introduced the house system [into the school] and they've chosen [one of] the house names to be Edwards (reads the email), 'you are inspirational... for our young people.' So stuff like that... makes me know that I'm on the right path... You [get inspired by] people that you know... or see and [they are from where you are from]... because then you will be more inspired to start your own thing. So legacy for me means setting up great foundations for others... to be inspired and to be able to do whatever it is in their field... even if it's outside of business or entrepreneurship...

TSF: When you started SBTV was [it] about shining a light on people with talent in your community?

JE: Yeah, definitely.

TSF: What was the pull for you to start [SBTV]?

JE: I think the main thing was just being... frustrated with mainstream media platforms not featuring the talent that I wanted... And my mates being like, 'how do we get our videos [out there]?'... So I wanted to create my own sort of thing... So it was problem solving I would say. It was born out of the frustration of my mates and wanting to problem solve for them... that was basically why I started my own platform...There wasn't a clear route of how [musicians could] get on.

TSF: When you think back to those times with SBTV did you imagine it becoming what it's become? And did you imagine yourself at the time being the person you are today?...

JE: No, not really. But... now... when things happen? It just reinforces it in my mind. But when I first started,

I never I never really thought I'd get to where I am. It's always… reaffirming… sometimes I might have a moment where I'm (discouraged sigh) and then I'll get something like, for example, [the Lee Manor Secondary school house being named after me] and I will be like, 'oh shit'…

TSF: It all leads into something.

JE: Yeah and… it's not like I'm aiming for stuff… I… go with the flow and just keep it humble and keep my head down and try and work as much as much as possible…

TSF: Not to get spiritual… but I always think that entrepreneurship and being a leader… is a gift that we're born with, whether we know it or not, like some people speak and say that… they always felt that they were meant to lead or help people… But just like… the blessing of being able to sing [that your mum and sister have]… I think being a leader was born in you and obviously activated through frustration… So it's really interesting to hear that in reverse, where it's almost like, you're living through this destiny, and then all the small things come to affirm it, like the school wanting to name a house after you…

JE: When I think about it I've been in this since I was about like 15… So like, getting on now… I've always said to myself, 'what is my legacy?' So… what's my legacy in the next 5 to 10 years? And what I'm gonna do in these next 5 to 10 years, because… I feel like I'm halfway into a career like Darcus Beese, who's the president of Island Records [said] it's 20 years to a career. So, right now, I feel like I'm at a halfway point. I'm looking to… rebrand myself, get back into it, start doing more, getting more active with film and whatnot… I'm at a very good place in my mind. I'm excited. I'm excited to wake up each day and attack each day. Like there were times where I'd wake up, and I just feel like, 'ah I can't be asked' but at the moment I am focused…

TSF: I think… we take for granted that thing that you described… people say it's anxiety. I describe mine as anxiety, or depression … that is something that all successful people feel? You're 15 years… would be some people's 30. So it's very easy for you to feel like, 'ah I'm 30—what have I done? Where am I going? What do I do?' without actually acknowledging how many mountains you've moved.

JE: …its good though… well good and bad. It keeps you on it and focused.

TSF: …That's the reason why you're able to now rebrand, pivot and focus on other ways to be impactful. Yeah, which is so good. Where do you see the next 15? going then? Is there anything that you want to do or that you've got your eyes on?

JE: [Giving back to the community] …the three places that are close to my heart are Acton, Luton and St Vincent. And like, obviously, I've set up like Delve, which is [an organisation that] repurposes old youth community centres, which I've been working on with

Google and the Wellcome Trust. ...I'd like to scale that up outside of Acton [and do it] across different boroughs in London, and in Luton and St. Vincent as well. [I want to] help young people in those areas to realise their full potential, but then also create some real good content and build myself as a director. That's what I'd like to do over the next five to 10 years.

TSF: I like the idea of going back to the community

JE: Yeah, I've been doing it already in Acton and now it's time to branch out.

TSF: What type of things would you want to reach out with? Would it be entrepreneurship for young people? Or a mix of [things]?

JE: Anything a young person wants? I try to keep it as broad as possible because my life is broad. It's about trying to keep as broad as possible. If a young person comes to me and says, 'I want to be a lawyer', I will look into getting a contract from a lawyer. If they're saying 'I want to be an accounts payable manager,' I'll look at trying to fing that... Obviously, when I first started a lot of young people were like , 'oh is it just going to be about music, though,' but kids are interested in [many other things too]. [Even though] I'm known for music [I'll do] anything to help [in other areas]...

TSF: ...The fact that you're willing to [use] your social mobility for young people, I think is what makes what you're going to do in the next 5,10 15,20 years so impactful...

JE: Fingers crossed all I can do is hope and pray but I don't pray (laughs)… my family is very religious… they pray for me…

TSF: You've got nuff protection when you have that kind of power of the hand behind you (laughs)…

JE: Yeah it's crazy the power of that… [my family] blesses me and I know I've got that blessing. So I feel like I've got that part of me. If I go through a hard time, I can go and speak to my aunty Pam and she [gives] me words of wisdom.

TSF: Well, thank you so much for this really, really fantastic conversation… Thank you. I really enjoyed it. It's been so enjoyable. …thank you so much for your contributions… they are not unnoticed, we really appreciate you.

ACKNOWLEDGEMENTS

There are not enough words in the English language that could describe the amount of love I have for the people listed below that are due more than an acknowledgement, but I will give it a try.

Mi corazón, mum. Thank you for loving me endlessly, and being there through every laugh and tear. You have dedicated your life in service of others, and it is that divinity within you that I try to emulate every single day.

Lots of light to my friends, especially Andrea and Becky who in moments of doubt have lifted my spirits with their charm and care. They say that your friends are the family you can choose, I feel blessed to have the opportunity to call you my chosen sisters.

Thank you to Magdalene Abraha, the visionary behind the *A Quick Ting On* series. This has truly been the hardest thing I have ever worked on, and having you there, unjudging and supporting, has meant the world. Being part of this series, being part of this making of history is an honour, so thank you! I hope those who get the privilege of reading all the *AQTO* works are as inspired as I have been getting to work with you all.

Lastly, to every little Black girl who serves as my reflection, I pray that all you have achieved and survived so far serves as testimony to the greatness that has always existed within you—no person or obstacle can obstruct the wondrous fate you are due.

ABOUT THE AUTHOR

Tskenya-Sarah is an award-winning diversity, inclusion and sustainability specialist. Over the past nine years, Tskenya has implemented equitable and profitable strategic roadmaps that ensure diversity and inclusion underpins all functional areas of businesses across global public, private and third sectors spanning the global regions of APAC/EMEA/LAD/NA. She has acted as an advisor to His Majesty King Charles III and the government through her work with the Prince's Trust International Youth Entrepreneurship Board. Tskenya is also an award winning business owner and has been featured in Forbes, Vogue and more.

Tskenya continues to advocate for the further representation of neurodiverse, disabled and minoritised groups within businesses, entrepreneurship and venture capital. Person-centric, dynamic and charismatic, Tskenya brings a consistent intersectional lens to everything she does.

A Quick Ting On: Black British Business is Tskenya's debut book.

ENDNOTES

CHAPTER 1

1   Exploring the Entrepreneurial Society Institutions, Behaviors and Outcomes, 2017, p.25

2   Brit(ish): On Race, Identity and Belonging Afua Hirsch, 2018, p. 33

3   Frantz Fanon's 'Black Skin, White Masks', New Interdisciplinary Essays, Max Silverman 2017, p.9

4   Women's Under-Representation in the Engineering and Computing Professions: Fresh Perspectives on a Complex Problem by Kathleen Buse, Catherine Hill, Romila Singh, 2018, p.118

5   McKinsey and Company Diversity Wins Report, 2020

CHAPTER 2

1   Carroll, Rory. 'New book reopens old arguments about slave raids on Europe.' *The Guardian*, 11 March 2004

2   Sandhu, Sukhdev. 'The First Black Britons.' *BBC History*, 17 February 2011

3   Sandhu, Sukhdev. 'London Calling.' *Architectural Association School of Architecture*, no. 49, 2003, pp. 50—56. *JSTOR*

4   Ibid.

5   Sandhu, Sukhdev. 'The First Black Britons.' BBC History, 17 February 2011

6   Fryer, Peter. *Staying Power: The History of Black People in Britain*, Pluto Press, 2010, p. 162

7   Kaufmann, Miranda. 'Out of Africa: Stories of pioneering black women in Early Modern England.' *University of London*, 2018

8   The National Archives. 'Introduction : Arriving in Britain.' *The National Archives*

9   Hume, David. *Essays—Moral, Political and Literary*, Liberty Fund Inc; 2nd Revised edition, 1987, p. 252.

10   Eze, Emmanuel C. Achieving Our Humanity : The Idea of the Postracial Future, Routledge, 2001, p. 102.

11   Mamata, Bidisha SK. 'Tudor, English and black—and not a slave in sight.' *The Guardian*, 29 October 2017

12   Black Tudors Miranda Kaufmann p. 8

13   Ibid, p.9

14   Encounter Images in the Meetings Between Africa and Europe by Mai Palmberg, 2001, p .103

15   Black Africans in Renaissance Europe by Thomas Foster Earle, T. F. Earle, K. J. P. Lowe · 2005, p.39

16   Ibid.

17   Ibid.

18   Ibid, p.109

19   Encyclopedia of African-American Culture and History, David L. Smith, p. 847

20   Letters of the Late Ignatius Sancho, an African by Ignatius Sancho and Joseph Jekyll, 1784, p.202

21   Student Encyclopedia of African Literature by G. D. Killam p. 277

22   Unchained Voices: An Anthology of Black Authors in the English-Speaking World of the Eighteenth Century by Vincent Carretta, p 107

23   Access to History: Britain 1783-1885 by Benjamin Armstrong, 2020, p.4

24   Lest We Forget: Remembrance & Commemoration by Maggie Andrews and Nigel Hunt, 2011, p 111

25   Davis, Miles. 'Joseph Emidy: From slave fiddler to classical violinist.' *The BBC*, 21 June 2015

26   Ibid.

27   Ibid.

28   Ibid.

29   Emidy, Joseph Antonio. 'The extraordinary tale of African slave Joseph Emidy who became a Cornwall celebrity.' *Cornwall Live*, 7 March 2020

30   Ibid.

31   'Cesar Picton.' *Explore Surrey's Past*, 2012

32   Ibid.

33   BBC History. 'The Prosperous Silk Weaver.' *BBC History*, 9 November 2017, p. 37

34   Ibid.

35   Whitchurch Silk Mill. 'The Story of Reasonable Blackman.' *Whitchurch Silk Mill*, 2021

36   Ibid.

37   BBC History. 'The Prosperous Silk Weaver.' *BBC History*, 9 November 2017, p. 37

38   McDowell, Linda. 'How Caribbean migrants helped to rebuild Britain.' *The British Library*, 2018

39   Joshua, Harris. *A Circle of Five*, Jacaranda Books, 2020, p. 35.

40   Ibid.

41   McDowell, Linda. 'How Caribbean migrants helped to rebuild Britain.' *The British Library*, 2018

42   Ibid.

43   Sky. 'WW2—REBUILDING LONDON.' *Sky History*, 2017

44   Phillips, Riaz. *British Food Wouldn't Be the Same without the Windrush Generation*. VICE, 2018

45   Phillips, Riaz. 'BLACK HISTORY MONTH: THE AFRO-CARIBBEAN WOMEN WHO CHANGED BRITAIN'S FOOD MAP.' *The Fawcett Society*, 2017

46   Urban, Mike. "Keep Brixton White'—shocking pamphlet from 1955 London County Council Elections.' *Brixton Buzz*, 2014

47   Hinds, Donald. 'Claudia Jones and the 'West Indian Gazette." *The Institute of Race Relations*, 2008

48   Ibid.

49   Past In The Present. 'Remembering the Windrush Generation in Notting Hill.' *Past In The Present : Travelling The World, Discovering The Past*, 2018

50   The City Speaks. 'Notting Hill Carnival.' *The City Speaks*, 2012

51   Ibid.

52   The Voice. 'About Us.' *The Voice*, 2021

53   Ibid.

54   Windrush Foundation. 'Val McCalla.' *Windrush Pioneers & Champions*, Windrush Foundation, 2019, p. 142.

55   Ibid.

56   'Flamingo magazine, September 1961.' *The British Library*

57   Ibid.

58   Ibid.

59   Chambers, Eddie. 'Rasta This and Dreadlocks That.' *Roots & Culture : Cultural Politics In The Making Of Black Britain*, I.B Tauris, 2017, p. 90.

60   Williams, Paul H. 'The Dyke, Dryden and Wade Story (Finale).' *The Jamaican Gleaner*, 22 February 2010

61   Ibid.

62   Windrush Foundation. 'LEN DYKE, DUDLEY DRYDEN & ANTHONY WADE.' *Windrush Pioneers & Champions*, Windrush Foundation, 2019, p. 148

63   Melan Mag. "Splinters Salon? It was like the MOTOWN of Afro hair': Derek DeCutter.' *Melan Mag*, 2018

64   Chabo, Elena. 'This is the new chapter of the black hair industry, and it's pretty powerful.' *Stylist Magazine*, 2019

65   Phillips, Mike. 'Oswald Denniston—Pillar of the Brixton community who arrived on the Windrush.' *The Guardian*, 17 February 2000

66   Windrush Foundation. 'OSWALD DENNISTON.' *Windrush pioneers & champions*, 2018, p. 45

67   Ibid.

68   Ibid.

69   Gregory, Ruby. 'How Britain's first Black radio station began on a Brixton estate and grew to be one of the largest in the UK.' *My London*, 2021

70   Ibid.

71   Classic FM. 'How the Windrush generation changed British music and arts forever.' *Classic FM*, 22 June 2020

72   Bradley, Lloyd. 'Sound systems.' *The British Library*, 4 October 2018

73   Ibid.

74   Ibid.

CHAPTER 3

1   British Business Bank, UK VC & Female Founders report, 2019

2   *Black Male Outsider: Teaching as a Pro-Feminist Man* By Gary L. Lemons. p. 181

3   Kniggendorf, Anne. 'The barriers to funding equality persist for black women.' *Ewing Marion Kauffman Foundation*

4   *Do Better: Spiritual Activism for Fighting and Healing* by Rachel Ricketts, 2021. p 270

5   State of Women Business Report, American Express, 2019

6   Ibid.

7   Friedberg, Suzanne. 'African Market Women and Economic Power: The Role of Women in African Economic Development.' *Journal of Political Ecology*, vol. 4, 1997

8   Clark, Gracia. 'African Market Women, Market Queens, and Merchant Queens.' *Oxford Research Encyclopedias*, 2018

9   Ibid.

10   Friedberg, Suzanne. 'African Market Women and Economic Power: The Role of Women in African Economic Development.' *Journal of Political Ecology*, vol. 4, 1997

11   Clark, Gracia. 'African Market Women, Market Queens, and Merchant Queens.' *Oxford Research Encyclopedias*, 2018

12   Ibid.

13   Friedberg, Suzanne. 'African Market Women and Economic Power: The Role of Women in African Economic Development.' *Journal of Political Ecology*, vol. 4, 1997

14   Clark, Gracia. 'African Market Women, Market Queens, and Merchant Queens.' *Oxford Research Encyclopedias*, 2018

15   Giving a Voice to the Voiceless: Four Pioneering Black Women Journalists By Jinx Coleman Broussard p.3

16   In Praise of Black Women: Ancient African queens, By Simone Schwarz-Bart, André Schwarz-Bart, foreword

17   Market Women: Black Women Entrepreneurs--past, Present, and Future by Cheryl A Smith, p. 15

18   Ibid, p.16

19   Diversity Beyond Gender Report By Erika Brodnock, Extend Ventures

20   Mitchell, Angela, and Kennise Herring. *What the Blues*

Is All About: Black Women Overcoming Stress and Depression. Penguin Putnam Inc., 1988

21   Jordan-Zachery, Julia S. *Black Women, Cultural Images and Social Policy*, Routledge, 2010, p. 38.

22   Kaur, Sanmeet. 'Sex and Power Report.' *Fawcett Society*, Fawcett Society, 2020

23   Baroness McGregor-Smith. 'Race in the workplace: The McGregor-Smith review.' *GOV.UK*, Department for Business, Energy & Industrial Strategy, 28 February 2017

24   The Trades Union Congress. 'TUC: BME women are twice as likely to be in insecure jobs as white workers | TUC.' *Trades Union Congress*, 28 October 2020

25   Reiners, Bailey, and Hal Koss. '57 Diversity In the Workplace Statistics In 2022.' *Built In*, 21 October 2021

CHAPTER 4

1   Full Surrogacy Now: Feminism Against Family, Sophie Lewis, p.200

2   Women's Suffrage: The Complete Guide to the Nineteenth Amendment by Tiffany K. Wayne, p. 274

3   Abraha 'Intersectional feminism: Why class, sexuality, ethnicity, race and ability must be taken into account when fighting for equality for all women.' *The Independent*, 4 September 2015

4   Ibid.

5   Ibid.

6   Burrell, Lynda-Louise. 'Pearl Alcock—The art of living.' *Black History Month*, 2 October 2021

7   Ibid.

8   Theil, Michele. 'The secret London gay bar that opened opposite a pub that banned black people.' *My London*, 21 February 2021

9   Murphy, Dr Gillian. 'The Black Lesbian and Gay Centre.' *LSE Blogs*, 2016

10   Ibid.

]11   The LGBT Market: How Much is the Pink Pound Worth?, Springer

12   Setterington, Ken. *Branded by the Pink Triangle*. Second Story Press, 2013

13   Schwartz, Daniel B. *Ghetto: The History of a Word*. Harvard University Press, 2019

14   Peace News for Nonviolent Revolution. 'Peace News for Nonviolent Revolution.' no. 2260-2283, 1986.

15   Ackroyd, Peter. *Queer City: Gay London from the Romans to the Present Day*. Chatto & Windus, 2017.

16   Controversies in Contemporary Advertising by Kim Bartel Sheehan, p. 249

17   LGBT Identification Rises to 5.6% in Latest Estimate by Jeffery Jones

18   LGBT-Inclusive Companies Are Better at 3 Big Things by Sylvia Ann Hewlett and Kenji Yoshino

19   Hardin III, Floyd H. 'African American gay male entrepreneurs: a study of enabling and inhibiting factors impacting entrepreneurial success.' *Pepperdine University*, 2016. *Pepperdine.*

20   Ibid.

21   Ibid.

22   Ibid.

23   Ibid.

24   Ibid.

25   Carlisle, Madeleine. 'A New Crowdsourcing App Hopes to Serve as the 'Green Book' for LGBTQ+ People of Color.' *Time Magazine*, 18 May 2021,

26   Ibid.

27   Queer   Intercultural   Communication: The Intersectional Politics of Belonging in and Across Differences by Shinsuke Eguchi, p. 230

CHAPTER 5

1   Daley, James. *Great Speeches by African Americans: Frederick Douglass, Sojourner Truth, Dr. Martin Luther King, Jr., Barack Obama, and Others*. Dover Publications Inc, 2006.

2   Ibid.

3   Umoja, Akinyele, et al., editors. *Black Power Encyclopedia : From 'Black Is Beautiful' to Urban Uprisings*. Greenwood Publishing Group Inc, 2018

4   Ebony Magazine. *EBONY*, July 1988, p. 20.

5   Paul, Heike. *The Myths That Made America: An Introduction to American Studies*, Transcript Verlag, 2014, p. 213.

6   Biography. 'Madam C.J. Walker.' *Biography*, https:// www.biography.com/inventor/madam-cj-walker. Accessed 25 October 2021.

7   Ibid.

8   Ibid.

9   Ibid.

10   Black Enterprise Magazine. *Black Enterprise Magazine*, December 1989, p. 90.

11   Adegoke, Yomi. "It's About Ownership': The Politics of Running a Black Hair Shop.' *VICE*, 14 June 2016

12   Don't Touch My Hair By Emma Dabiri, 2019, p.99

13   Haircare market value in Great Britain 2009-2020 by M. Ridder, Aug 9, 2021, Statista

14   Muttucumaru, Ayesha. 'NOT FAIR: SUPERDRUG STEPS UP BUDGET BEAUTY GAME FOR DARKER SKIN TONES.' *Get The Gloss*, 2016

15   Ibid.

16   Helm, Jessica S., et al. 'Measurement of endocrine disrupting and asthma-associated chemicals in hair products used by Black women.' *Environmental Research*, vol. 165, 2018, p. 449. *Research Gate*

17   Ibid.

18   Scottham, Krista Maywalt. *What We Tell Our Sons and Daughters: Parent-child Race Socialization Among African American Adolescents*, University of Michigan, 2011, p. 94

19   Rosenberg, Lynn, et al. 'Hair product use and breast cancer incidence in the Black Women's Health Study.' Edited by Patricia F. Coogan. *Carcinogenesis*, vol. 42, no. 7, 2021, pp. 924–930

20   Breastcancer.org. 'Untangling Link Between Hair Relaxers and Breast Cancer Risk in Black Women.' *Breastcancer. org*, 2021

21   Silent Spring Institute. 'Hair products for Black women contain mix of hazardous ingredients.' *Silent Spring Institute*, 10 April 2018

22   Ibid.

23   Ross, Lawrence C. 'The Ways of Black Folks.' Dafina—Op/nla Titles, 2003, p. 24

24   Bristol, Jr., Douglas W. *Knights of the Razor: Black Barbers in Slavery and Freedom*, Johns Hopkins University Press, 2015, p. 229

25   Mills, Quincy T. 'Cutting Along the Color Line: Black Barbers and Barber Shops in America.' University of Pennsylvania Press, 2013, 61, 229, 173.

26   Ibid.

27   Cutting Along the Color Line: Black Barbers and Barber Shops by Quincy T. Mills, 2013, p 140

28   Ibid.

29   Barbershops, Bibles, and BET Everyday Talk and Black Political Thought By Melissa Victoria Harris-Lacewell, 2010, p.200

30   Jeffries, Judson L., et al. *African American Culture: An Encyclopedia of People, Traditions, and Customs Volume 3*, Greenwood Publishing Group Inc, 2020, p. 62

31   Feldman, Lynne, and John N. Ingham. *African-American Business Leaders: A Biographical Dictionary*, Greenwood, 1993, p. 329.

32   Simpson, Menelik. 'Trips to the barbershop taught me how to be a man.' *METRO*, 29 June 2017

33   Oppenheim, Naomi. 'Winston Whyte's Barber Shop Trial.' *The British Library*, 29 November 2017

34   Oppenheim, Naomi. 'Winston Whyte's Barber Shop Trial.' *The British Library*, 29 November 2017

35   Donnell, Alison. 'Hairdressing.' *Companion to Contemporary Black British Culture*, Routledge, 2013, p. 134.

36   Lewis, Sonja. 'SIXTY YEARS ON: HOW IS AFRO HAIR IN UK?' *Sonja Lewis*, 2012

37   'Picture This.' *The Politics of Heritage: The Legacies of Race*, edited by Roshi Naidoo and Jo Littler, Routledge, 2005, p. 178.

38   Ibid.

39   Donnell, Alison. 'Hairdressing.' *Companion to Contemporary Black British Culture*, Routledge, 2013, p. 134.

40   Ibid.

41   'Picture This.' *The Politics of Heritage: The Legacies of Race*, edited by Roshi Naidoo and Jo Littler, Routledge, 2005, p. 178.

CHAPTER 6

1   Gen Z minors: Born after 2000, Gen Z adults: Born

1995–2000, Millennials: Born 1983–1994, Gen X: Born 1964–1982, Boomers: Born 1943–1963, Silent: Born before 1943

2   Epsilon, *Digital Shopping Tool Impact Study 2015*

3   Synchony, Balancing Multi-Generational Retail Strategies Winning over Millennials without losing Boomers

4   Ibid.

5   The Times. 'Boohoo: fashion giant faces 'slavery investigation.'' *The Times*, 5 July 2020

6   The Telegraph. 'Why more than half of UK businesses are planning to increase spend on sustainability.' *The Telegraph*, 8 November 2019

7   Ibid.

8   Latham, Katherine. 'Has coronavirus made us more ethical consumers?' *BBC*, 14 January 2021

9   The Telegraph. 'Why more than half of UK businesses are planning to increase spend on sustainability.' *The Telegraph*, 8 November 2019

10   Laughland, Pamela, and Tima Bansal. 'THE TOP TEN REASONS WHY BUSINESSES AREN'T MORE SUSTAINABLE.' *Ivey Business Journal*, 2011

11   Ibid.

12   'UK Ethical Consumer Markets Report.' *Ethical Consumer*, 2020.

13   Ibid.

14   Ethical Consumer Markets Report. 'Ethical Consumer Markets Report 2020.' *Ethical Consumer*, 1 December 2020

15   Ibid.

16   Adeniji, Adedoyin. 'The unintended consequences of #SupportBlackBusiness.' *VOX*, 3 September 2020

17   Adeniji, Adedoyin. 'The unintended consequences of #SupportBlackBusiness.' *VOX*, 3 September 2020

18   Ibid.

19   Yelp Economic Average, Increased Consumer Interest

in May Correlates with COVID-19 Hot Spots in June, 2020

20   Self-Employment, Family Background, and Race by Michael Hout and Rosen Harvey, 2000, p. 670-692

CHAPTER 7

1   British Business Bank, Alone together: Entrepreneurship and diversity in the UK, 2020

2   Ibid.

3   Ibid.

4   Ibid.

5   Ibid.

6   Ibid.

7   Costa, MaryLou. 'Putting Black-owned businesses in the spotlight.' *Raconteur*, Raconteur, 28 July 2020

8   Office of National Statistics, Effects of taxes and benefits on UK household income: financial year ending 2019, 2020

9   Ibid.

10   Ibid.

11   Azeez, Walé. 'Black British entrepreneurs rely on foreign investment while home funds look away.' *CNN*, 16 December 2021, https://edition.cnn.com/2021/12/16/tech/black-entrepreneurs-uk-racism/index.html. Accessed 30 May 2022.

12   Hossein, Caroline Shenaz. 'Money Pools in the Americas: The African Diaspora's Legacy in the Social Economy.' *Forum for Social Economics*, vol. 45, no. March Issue, 2016

13   Ardener, Shirley, and Sandra Burman. *Money-Go-Rounds : The Importance of ROSCAs for Women*. Routledge, 1996

14   Hossein, Caroline Shenaz. 'Money Pools in the Americas: The African Diaspora's Legacy in the Social

Economy.' *Forum for Social Economics*, vol. 45, no. March Issue, 2016

15   Office of National Statistics, Household wealth by ethnicity, Great Britain, 2020

16   https://www.lloydsbankinggroup.com/media/press-releases/2021/lloyds-bank/majority-of-black-business-owners-lack-trust-in-banks-to-support-their-business-goals.html

17   The Capitalist and the Activist: Corporate Social Activism by Tom Lin, 2021, p. 90

18   Accelerator Programme—A business accelerator support start-ups through investment, mentoring and training.

19   https://www.morganstanley.com/press-releases/expansion-of-multicultural-innovation-lab-in-london

20   Collins, Eric. 'Black businesses are in crisis.' Sifted, 19 June 2020

CHAPTER 8

1   Bounds, Andy. 'Coronavirus claims thousands of UK businesses.' *Financial Times*, 19 April 2020

2   Office for National Statistics, Coronavirus and the impact on output in the UK economy: June 2020

3   Olarewaju, Tolu, and Jagannadha Pawan Tamvada. 'Black and minority ethnic businesses need support to weather the pandemic.' *The Conversation*, 30 October 2020

4   Olarewaju, Temitayo, and Tolu Olarewaju. 'Ethnic Poverty: Causes, Implications, and Solutions.' *Encyclopedia of the UN Sustainable Development Goals*, Springer, 2021

5   Clowes, Ed, et al. 'Black and Asian businesses could not access Covid support, MPs find.' *The Telegraph*, 8 October 2020

6   'Cost of Living Crisis—People Like Us.' *People Like Us*, People Like Us, 2022,

7   Ibid.

8   Ibid.

9   Ibid.

10   Fraser, Douglas. 'Business confidence is falling, says Natwest boss.' *BBC*, 26 May 2022

11   'Business of change report 2022 | wellness & empowerment.' *PayPal*, PayPal, 28 June 2022

CHAPTER 9

1   Sociologists Yaojun Li of Manchester University and Anthony Heath of Oxford University—Class Matters: A Study of Minority and Majority Social Mobility in Britain, 1982–2011, 2016, American Journal of Sociology 122(1):162-200

2   https://www.libdemvoice.org/clegg-lib-dem-social-mobility-commission-shatters-the-idea-that-britain-in-2009-is-a-free-and-fair-society-10117.html

3   https://www.gov.uk/government/news/class-privilege-remains-entrenched-as-social-mobility-stagnates

4   https://assets.publishing.service.gov.uk/government/uploads/system/uploads/attachment_data/file/798687/SMC_State_of_Nation_2018-19_Summary.pdf

5   https://www.transparentcollective.com/who-we-are.html#

6   llana Gershon, Down and Out in the New Economy: How People Find (or Don't Find) Work Today University of Chicago Press, March 2017

7   A Burst of Light: And Other Essays—Audre Lorde, p.91

8   Art Therapy for Social Justice: Radical Intersections by Savneet K. Talwar, 2018, p.131

9   Historical Dictionary of the Civil War and Reconstruction by William L. Richter, 2012, p. 443

10   The Slaves' Economy: Independent Production by Slaves in the Americas by Ira Berlin, Philip D. Morgan, 2016, p. 187

11   Encyclopedia of Hair: A Cultural History by Victoria Sherrow, 2006, p.17

CHAPTER 10

1   How Europe Underdeveloped Africa By Walter Rodney and Angela Davis p. 386